THE ANGEL OF MARYE'S HEIGHTS

Sergeant Richard Kirkland's Extraordinary
Deed at Fredericksburg

by Les Carroll

Published by:
Palmetto Bookworks
P.O. Box 11551
Columbia, SC 29211

Copyright © 1994 by

Lester T. Carroll, Jr.

All Rights Reserved

Manufactured in the United States of America by:

Palmetto Bookworks
P.O. Box 11551
Columbia, SC 29211

ISBN 0-9623065-7-6

To My Father

The Angel of Marye's Heights

Robert W. Wilson

Foreword
i

A sunken road and a wall of stone
v

For the slumbering guns awake to life
1

And the gray stone wall is ringed with fire
9

Again and again a new line forms
21

And then from out of the battle smoke
31

And into the presence of Kershaw brave
43

On the plains below the blue lines glow
53

Like Daniel of old in the lion's den
65

And I am sure in the Book of Gold
73

THE ANGEL OF MARYE'S HEIGHTS
82

Index
84

Richard Rowland Kirkland   The Angel of Marye's Heights

Foreword

Richard Kirkland was taken from this earth more than 130 years ago and to all but a small group of dedicated historians and supporters, his name is not well known. Today, most young people in South Carolina and even many in Kershaw County, where he was born and lived most of his 20 years, do not know who Richard Kirkland was or what he did. So when I began researching the Richard Kirkland story, my primary hope was to make his story accessible, especially to young people. I thought the students of today should know that the Civil War was more than just great generals and great battles, secession, states' rights, regional freedom and slavery. The Civil War was so much more, and writers, historians and photographers have done an unbelievable job of keeping the war fresh in the minds of our citizens. Yes, the war was violent and volatile. It produced great tragedy and incredible valor. The war created a setting in which ordinary young men performed extraordinary acts of courage and compassion.

Very little is known about Richard Kirkland, other than his brave deed at Fredericksburg, and small amounts of information about his youth and his death. But because there are such good records kept of Civil War participants, it was easy to recount, with some accuracy I hope, the battles in which Kirkland participated. In fashioning his story into what I hope is an interesting narrative, I at times simply researched those battles and the units to which Kirkland belonged, and placed him into the story. Kirkland was right in the middle of some of the most historical events in our country's history -- the siege of Fort Sumter, the Battles of Bull Run, Fredericksburg and Gettysburg.

My apologies to the historians and purists who want everything documented. For this short work, that would have been unreasonable, and impossible. In fact, several anecdotes in the book are based on stories people told me, tales that their fathers had told them, and their fathers' fathers had told them. (Or their mothers, of course). I asked where I could find out more about such information, and they would tell me that it's not written anywhere, it's just how the story has always been told in their family, generation after generation. That's good enough for me. The accounts of battles and historical events are my own expression of what happened, and what I thought Kirkland's involvement was at a specific place and time.

Most importantly, the purpose of the book, to tell about Kirkland at Fredericksburg, Virginia in December, 1862, is historically documented. We know Kirkland performed a great deed at Fredericksburg and I wanted young people, and the not so young, to read that and know his story.

Lastly, I am not a historian, and have only recently begun to study the Civil War with some commitment. I started out as an enthusiast, and haven't advanced to the next level yet. So, any errors in my conclusions or descriptions are strictly accidental, and for them, I apologize.

My thanks go to the following people for their help: First, to Alexander B. Morrison, a general authority of The Church of Jesus Christ of Latter-day Saints, who put me onto this story with a brief mention of Kirkland in a sermon to Mormon youth in 1993. Morrison was speaking about service to others, and cited Kirkland as a superb example of selfless service to his fellowman. Hopefully some of the young people who heard Morrison's talk remember it. I certainly do.

Joe Matheson and the rest of the staff at the Camden Archives were a tremendous help in my research, as were Dotsy Boineau and the staff at the Confederate Museum and Relic Room and the staff of the South Caroliniana Library in Columbia. Angie Soots at the South Carolina State Library helped get the word out about the book. Hugh McLaurin put me onto some leads early in my search, and helped me get together with Gary Baker, whom I thank for editing and publishing this story, turning my manuscript into an attractive book, and my dream into reality.

I appreciate the skill of Steven Long, who created the maps for the book and Ron Chapiesky for his unique conception of Kirkland's plea to General Kershaw.

Robert W. Wilson painted a stirring portrait of Kirkland about ten years ago, and then graciously gave permission for me to make his work the cover of the book. It certainly makes an attractive dust jacket, and my thanks go to Mr. Wilson for his assistance and skills as an artist.

Ronald Seagrave and the rest of the staff at the Sergeant Kirkland's Museum and Historical Society in Fredericksburg, Virginia, reviewed the manuscript and offered photos and much - needed historical details.

Thanks also to Mark Baker for the typesetting and design of the book.

Richard Kirkland is one of our heroes. Somewhere in the heaven of war heroes and courageous soldiers, he's up there. May he be remembered.

-- Les Carroll

" A sunken road and a wall of stone
And Cobb's grim line of gray
Lay still at the base of Marye's hill
On the morn of a winter's day."

Prologue

The War Between the States, also known as the American Civil War, demanded the lives of many of the country's bravest, best men and boys. It is important that Americans everywhere, young and old, Northerners and Southerners, remember those who led the armies, and those who fought in the armies. From one of the darkest eras in our country's history, many heroes emerged. Some of the heroes are well known, like Generals Ulysses S. Grant, Robert E. Lee, James Longstreet, Joshua L. Chamberlain and Thomas "Stonewall" Jackson.

But most of the heroes were common soldiers -- privates, sergeants, lieutenants and captains, who performed many of the daring exploits that made their generals famous. These very ordinary men often accomplished extraordinary acts of valor and compassion. And so today, more than a century later, it's still important to remember those men and their deeds, and honor their memories.

Richard Kirkland was one of the men who performed one of those memorable acts of uncommon valor. His actions in battle have been summarized in ballads, journalism and the visual arts. But to many, he is still unknown. It is the hope of the author that this brief account will revive and memorialize the gallant actions, courage and compassion of Richard Rowland Kirkland, who was known to the Union soldiers at Fredericksburg, Virginia as *The Angel of Marye's Heights*.

Richard Kirkland was a Southern farm boy. He never led an army into battle. He went into battle with the army. He was one of the men asked to fight the war, for a cause he personally believed in. And those who led him applauded his brave, humane, selfless service. His young friends spoke and wrote of him with the highest regard.

The name of Richard Rowland Kirkland will never go down in history with the great Civil War leaders, like the great generals, whose heart-wrenching decisions won or lost battles. And yet, Kirkland is one of the war's cherished heroes. He carved his name into history with dedicated, humble service for two fierce years -- and one singular act of remarkable boldness and sympathy. Then, like thousands of the best young men of his generation, he too, fell at the hands of enemy brothers.

Kirkland left for others the task of telling his story. But he provided one grand event: two daring hours on the frozen fields of Fredericksburg, where he demonstrated to those around him just what kind of soldier and person he was, and why his name is still remembered today.

For the slumbering guns awake to life
And the screaming shell and ball
From the front and flanks crash through the ranks
And leave them where they fall.

As a young man, Richard Rowland Kirkland was just about like every other rural Southern boy who lived in the early part of 1861. He was loyal to the South and intimately dedicated to his home state of South Carolina, where he was born and raised, and where his forefathers planted deep family and community roots. Young Kirkland was certain that his state's cause, embraced by his friends, family and political leaders, was just and right. So, there was really no doubt what course his life would take. His own home state of South Carolina helped carve the path that would change the United States forever.

In December, 1860, the South Carolina General Assembly voted unanimously to secede from the Union and seek independence from the United States of America. Other Southern states vowed to follow. And, when his own beloved South Carolina broke away from the United States, the fate of Richard Kirkland, and thousands of Southern boys just like him, was appointed. Many boys and men would die, and their names would go unspoken, except by family members and friends. But Kirkland would make his mark in a most extraordinary way, during his second year at war.

Immediately after the decision to secede from the Union, South Carolina's Governor Francis W. Pickens called on the state's military leaders to begin raising troops. These men would be assembled, trained and prepared for war. They would be led by distinguished citizens and former officers of the United States, many trained at West Point or the South Carolina Military Academy. They had fought under the American flag. Many of their friends and comrades from the North were on the other side. But now the soldiers of the South would take up arms to protect their states against the Federal government of the United States. Their cause was emotional and explosive.

Richard Kirkland answered the call of duty on April 9, 1861, just one of thousands of young boys to enlist. He left his family's farm, his own dreams and aspirations, many of his friends, and his sweethearts. And with his companions from Kershaw County, Richard Kirkland went off, rifle in hand, to fight for his state, now part of his new country -- the Confederate States of America. He wouldn't fight so much for a country, but for his home, and the life his family had built.

Richard Kirkland was born in August, 1843, at the Flat Rock Township, just north of Camden, South Carolina, in Kershaw County. He lived twenty glorious years, but fell mortally wounded during a bloody battle of the Civil War. His life and military career were too short. It's impossible to predict what he might have accomplished had Richard survived the war, and lived on. That can be said about thousands of boys from the North and South. But it's to the benefit of others that Richard Kirkland left his mark in such a convincing way. His name lives on.

It was as if he were born to be a soldier. It was in his blood. He came from a family of soldiers, men who fought generation after generation to preserve hard-earned freedoms. At least ten of his ancestors fought on South Carolina soil during the American Revolutionary War, many within the sound of musket fire from their own homes and families. Richard's great-grandfather, Daniel Kirkland, had served in the American army as a supply sergeant during the battle of Camden in 1780.

Even in the middle of the 1800s, Camden was already a historic town. No fewer than three Revolutionary War battles had been fought within five miles of Richard Kirkland's home. Protecting their lands, property and tradition was something Kirkland family members did naturally. So, there was never any question about what young Richard would do when Governor Pickens issued the call. Richard Kirkland would become a soldier and defend his homeland.

Richard was the son of John A. and Mary Vaughn Kirkland, whose ancestors had built good lives on the fertile plantations in Kershaw County, South Carolina. Each generation had left to their children a life a little better than the one which had come before. John Kirkland had that goal too. But The War Between the States would change that.

Richard was the next youngest of seven children, six boys and a daughter, Caroline. Richard's mother died when he was just two years old, and he was raised by his father, older siblings and grand parents. The absence of his mother most surely affected Richard's young life, but also brought the family closer together. That family closeness instilled in Richard the qualities he would display later on the bloody battlefields of Virginia, Pennsylvania, Maryland and Georgia. John Kirkland did the best he could for his children. When the older children grew up and started families of their own, John Kirkland raised his three younger boys, whom he affectionately called Billy, Dickie and

Sammy. The little Kirkland boys were models in the community, little gentleman, clones of their good father. At Flat Rock Community Church and school, their friends and teachers loved them and spoke highly of all of John and Mary Kirkland's children.

Richard's brothers were James, Jesse, Dan, Billy and Sam. Jesse, Dan, and Billy joined the Confederate army when the call went out for volunteers, just as Richard had done. Sam traveled to Virginia for a short time, then returned home. Richard, Billy and Dan left their farms and went into battle within just a few months after joining up. Richard served in a different unit than his brothers, but they often saw each other between the early Civil War battles in Virginia, and even ate evening meals together on occasion. Dan and Billy served in a unit called the Kirkwood Rangers. Jesse served in the Seventh South Carolina Cavalry later.

Sam was about sixteen when war broke out at Fort Sumter, South Carolina. He traveled to Virginia to fight, or at least support the cause, but returned home early in the war. He joined the 22nd South Carolina Militia. This local militia unit was made up of residents who split up and served different communities. The militia helped maintain law and order, looked for run-away slaves and made sure the farmers planted food on their farms in addition to cotton. The members of the militia were considered unfit for duty in the regular Confederate army, for whatever the reason might be. In Sam Kirkland's case, his only reason was his young age.

Sam would later join the Seventh South Carolina Cavalry, after the death of his beloved brother, Richard. Some members of the Kirkland family thought that Sam only joined to avenge the death of his older brother. But after serving faithfully, young Sam would be the second Kirkland lost to this war. Although he was wounded, Sam survived the war, but was taken prisoner and sent to Point Lookout, Maryland. There Sam came down with a disease and died a year after the war ended, in the Spring of 1866. Like Richard, he left behind no wife and children. Richard's and Sam's young lives were cut way too short by the great war between brothers.

It is no wonder that Richard Kirkland was such a good soldier. A clever and creative boy, he helped work his family's three large land tracts. And he worked hard in other endeavors as well. At the age of 16, Richard and a friend helped a land surveyor map out a 288-acre farm near his father's plantations. Richard Kirkland worked hard on the job. He was good at the work and enjoyed it. The surveyor was very impressed with the work of Richard and his friend. When the job was complete, the surveyor included on the map of the property the names of "R. Kirkland and John Sill, Chain Carriers, 1859."

Richard did other surveying jobs and became very good at it. With the money he earned, he started buying farm tools at a local auction and planned for his own future. He was industrious, and liked to plan ahead. But Richard didn't hesitate when it came time to lay down his tools and drop his plow. Before his eighteenth birthday, young Richard left his family behind and joined the boys from Kershaw County in the war against the Union.

It must have been hard to leave home. There was plenty of work to do in upper Kershaw County and every strong body was needed. However, the spring crop of tobacco had been planted and everyone expected to be back before harvest time. The Kirkland family had three large tracts in the White Oak, Gum Swamp and Flat Rock regions of Kershaw County. The main farm was about twelve miles north from the town of Camden in Flat Rock Township. This is where Richard grew up, enjoying the usual adventures and duties of a Southern farm boy in the middle of the 1800s.

The Kirklands were well-known, middle-class citizens of Kershaw County, and became prominent by managing the hilly, gullied land with neat terraces. A little more than twenty slaves helped work the Kirkland's plantations. The area around the Kirkland land was scantily populated. Many of the local boys went off to serve with the Confederate armies during the Civil War. And scores of fine officers, including a half dozen who would eventually become generals, also took up leadership and command positions in the newly formed Confederate army. Unfortunately, way too many did not come home. Like hundreds of rural communities across the South, Kershaw County lost dozens and dozens of its brightest young sons to the war.

During the early excitement, when the clouds of war were still gathering, four of the Kirkland boys signed up to go off to war, including Richard. James, the oldest of the Kirkland boys, drew the short straw and was forced to stay home with his wife and children at his father's farm. Someone was needed to keep the farm operating and protect the women and children. James was not at all happy about staying home while his brothers joined the army. Like his brothers, he felt an obligation to fight for the cause of his state and the Confederacy. It didn't matter that staying away from the war would save his life, at least in the near-term. The young men of the South were willing to give up their lives for the cause.

But even though James Kirkland, and his father, John, stayed home, and away from the war's main activities, the war would eventually come to them and their plantations. Four years after Richard Kirkland and his brothers went off to war in 1861, Union General William T. Sherman and his men made their historic, destructive march through South Carolina. A few of the slaves on the Kirkland farm left and joined the Union soldiers, but several stayed on the farm. During this time, James Kirkland was forced to hide from Sherman's troops, some of which occupied the Kirkland house for three days and three nights in late February of 1865, while the Federals built bridges across the swollen Lynches River. The few slaves who stayed took food to James deep in the woods.

Sherman's men had left Columbia, the South Carolina capital, in flames just days earlier. They marched North, where local militiamen from the Camden area tried to slow the march of the Union soldiers. Several violent skirmishes broke out around Camden during the last days of February, 1865. Sherman sent his men to the farms to look for supplies and food. The Union soldiers also destroyed public property in Camden. North of the town, they ravaged the supplies on the Kirkland farms. The cured hams, bacon, barrels of molasses, flour and cornmeal, which had been stockpiled to feed Kirkland family members and slaves, were looted by Sherman's men. They left the region and marched on, leaving the Kirklands barren.

John Kirkland would never recover. He had spent all his money, and used all his credit to keep the farms operating in the absence of his sons. He borrowed Confederate money, and then later had to pay it back in Federal dollars, at terrible interest rates. The raid by Sherman's men was more than John Kirkland could handle. He lost all the possessions and security he had earned before the war, and in fact everything his family had built over several generations. He lost two of his fine sons to the war, and his oldest son tragically right after the war. James, who survived the raid of Sherman's army, was killed three months later on the Gum Swamp plantation, "felled by the hand of violence" on June 1, 1865. James Kirkland was 30 years old and left behind a wife and three children. Little more is known of the circumstances of his death, but James became the second of John Kirkland's sons to die. A year later, young Sam would be the third Kirkland boy to die within the span of three years. Two years after Sherman's march, John Kirkland died a poor and broken-hearted man, never regaining the social status achieved before the war. And he never got over the loss of his three young sons.

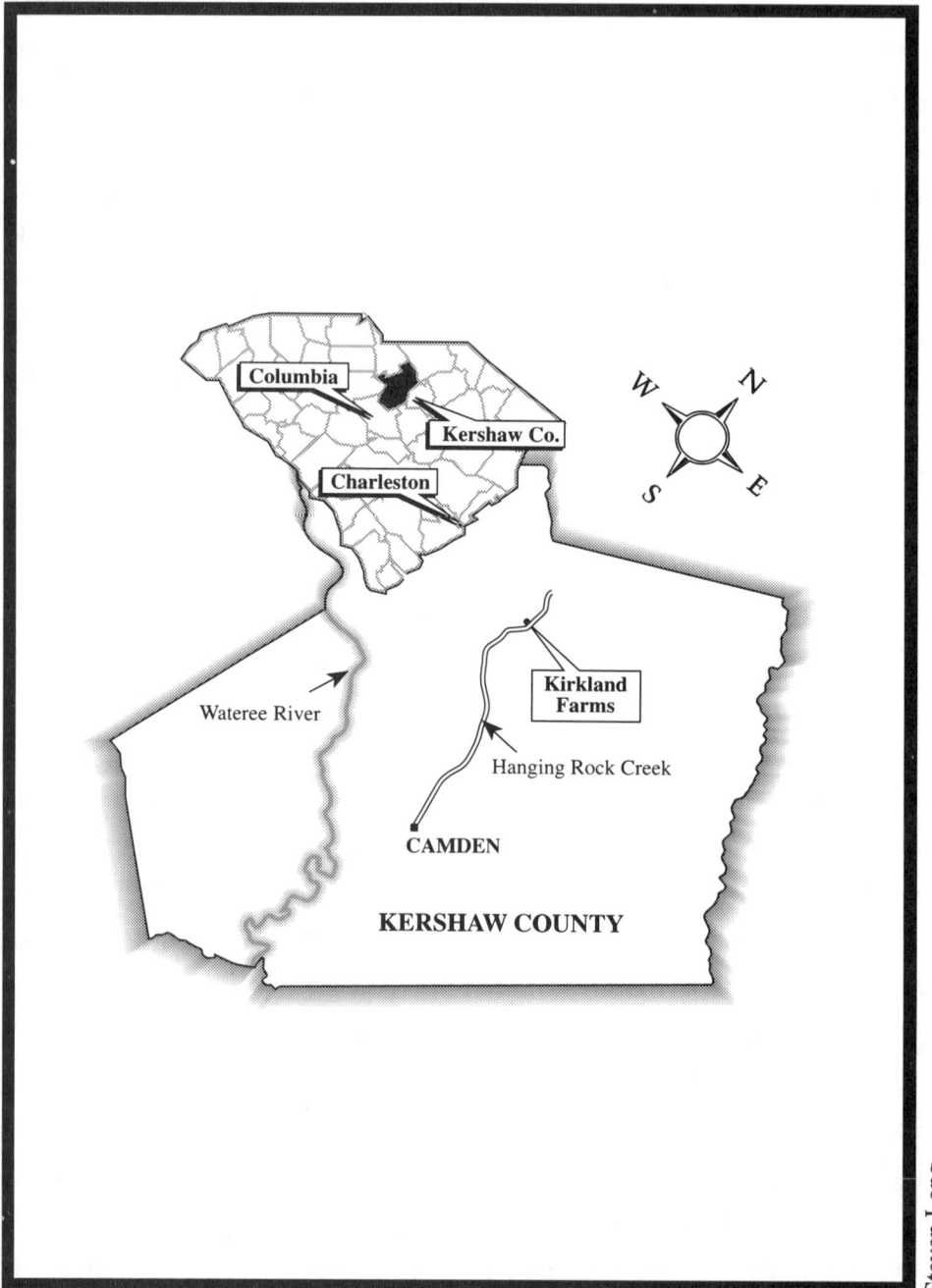

Map of South Carolina and Kershaw County

And the gray stone wall is ringed with fire
And the pitiless leaden trail
Drives back the foe to the plain below,
Shattered and crippled and frail.

Hoping to get into early action, Richard Kirkland rushed to Camden after the first call for volunteers, enlisting April 9, 1861, when he was not yet 18 years old. Richard signed up as a private in the Camden Volunteers, later formed as Company E, Second Regiment, South Carolina Volunteers, Infantry, under command of his friend and neighbor, Captain John D. Kennedy. Kennedy was Kirkland's commander during most of Richard's two years of service. The regimental commander of the Second Regiment, South Carolina Volunteers, was Colonel Joseph B. Kershaw, a prominent Kershaw attorney and military officer. Other local boys joined the Flat Rock Guards and the Kirkwood Rangers, two other units from the Kershaw County area. Kirkland's brothers went into the Kirkwood Rangers. Just days after the first muster of troops, Captain Kennedy issued this official report:

> *My company was accepted by Governor Pickens on the 8th day of January 1861, by virtue of authority vested in him to accept into service of the State of South Carolina ten thousand volunteers to constitute an armed force for said state, by act of General assembly of said state, passed in December 1860, was called into active service on 9th day of April 1861, remained in the state service till the 23rd day April when it was ordered to the state of Virginia, and is now in confederate service for the balance of the term of service due the state of South Carolina.*

> *John D. Kennedy*
> *Capt Camden Volunteers*
> *2nd Palmetto Regiment*
> *South Carolina Volunteers*

Private Richard Kirkland helped Captain Kennedy recruit others into their band of volunteers before leaving Kershaw County. Kirkland, like many young men, was enthusiastic about becoming a soldier. Most of the boys were. The young soldiers dreamed of glorious victories on the battlefields. They had no thoughts about the horrors of war they would later witness as they left Camden to the hearty cheers of the townspeople.

Richard and his pals left home immediately and traveled to Morris Island, near Charleston, South Carolina, where war was about to break out. Many of the South Carolina volunteer troops had gathered there because of the tension surrounding Fort Sumter. But the atmosphere was as festive as it was tense. There was a lot of excitement surrounding the secession and the rebellion of the Southern States. The people were independent and headstrong; they didn't want the United States to tell them what to do.

A Union artillery company occupied Fort Sumter, an island fortress in Charleston Harbor. The state government and people of South Carolina wanted the fort since it was in South Carolina territory. The governor wanted to decide the fate of the fort and not let that authority remain with the president of the United States. The bold Confederate commander, General Pierre G. T. Beauregard, warned the Federal troops to leave the fort. The Union commander of Fort Sumter was equally loyal and obedient to his government and refused to cooperate at first. But he had been cut off from supplies and had no way of protecting his men and the fort from the rebellious Southerners, who had formed a semi-circle of artillery around the fort on neighboring islands and the mainland.

When the Union commander, Major Robert Anderson, refused to relinquish command of the fortress, the Confederates opened fire at 4:30 a.m. on April 12th with a storm of artillery and cannon fire. For one full day and part of another, Southern artillerymen sent thousands of shot and shell into the fort's walls. Finally, Major Anderson knew that he could no longer hold Fort Sumter, and he agreed to surrender the fort to the men from South Carolina. The war between the Union and the Confederacy had begun.

Kirkland and his friends from Kershaw County arrived in Charleston during the bombardment of Fort Sumter. They were able to witness the attack but did not participate. The strike on Fort Sumter started a war that would not end until four years later. But at the time, no one believed that. Many Southerners thought, or perhaps hoped, that Fort Sumter would be the only battle. Some believed that the Union would realize that the South was willing to fight for its independence and the right to make and enforce its own laws. Many thought the Union would not challenge the South's determination to govern itself. But just the same, the Southern leaders knew in their hearts that war was just on the horizon. So they began preparing their volunteers for war.

Richard Kirkland's company and the other troops of Colonel Kershaw had gathered on Morris Island. They were a ragged band of zealous, young Southern boys, who didn't look much like a company of soldiers. Most of the volunteers did not have regular uniforms. And if they had uniforms, they had brought them from home, or received them from their fellow townspeople.

Many of these young soldiers, especially the volunteers, were not well equipped. In fact, they were very disorganized at first. Like the other volunteers, they had come from farms and plantations, colleges and factories. They had left their homes on short notice and joined the army of the new Confederacy. Most of them had no military experience. All they really had was a lot of heart, and a cause they felt was worth fighting for. And even dying for.

After Fort Sumter was surrendered by the Union, the young Southern soldiers wrote home and told their families about the unique experience. They called it a great victory, even though it really wasn't much of a battle at all. The politicians and military leaders called it a great victory also. But the real war would come later. And it would be nothing like the one-day bombardment of Fort Sumter.

The attack on Fort Sumter was led primarily by army veterans who had previously served in the United States army. Many had fought in many battles for the Union. For the most part, Confederate volunteers were a disorganized, unskilled army, not yet ready for war. They wore various types of uniforms, and some had brought with them primitive weapons not suited for engaging in battle against a large, well-equipped Union army.

The celebration that followed the capture of Fort Sumter quieted quickly. The generals knew the volunteers were badly in need of some immediate and intense military training. So in the days just after the siege of Fort Sumter, cadets from the Citadel, the military college in Charleston, were sent to the troop encampments. Their task was direct, but not simple. They would have to make soldiers out of the volunteers, and do it quickly. The cadets drilled the volunteer soldiers in combat skills and military discipline. The troops of Kershaw's Regiment, and the other South Carolina volunteers, were not prepared to fight. But they made up for their lack of training with determination and hard work. They were enthusiastic and picked up military techniques quickly. The training by the sharp Citadel cadets produced many funny and sometimes embarrassing moments. But the young troops kept their spirits high. And whether they were ready or not, the South Carolina volunteers were needed.

It was only through dedication and courage that these men became a determined fighting force, who would eventually fight and win battles of the Civil War against Union armies with fancy uniforms and new weapons. In fact, very soon after they were first gathered, Kershaw's Regiment, and the other volunteers, were ready to fight. And within weeks, Kershaw's men would play a key role in the South's first major victories of the Civil War in defense of Virginia. They left Charleston in mid-April and journeyed North by train to Richmond.

The trip to Virginia fascinated young Richard Kirkland and his comrades from South Carolina. The people of North Carolina and Virginia overwhelmed the soldiers with warm treatment, and hailed them as heroes. When the train passed through Wilmington, North Carolina and Petersburg, Virginia, crowds gathered to cheer the young soldiers. Many in the large welcoming group were charming young Southern ladies who shared tokens of friendship with the soldiers. The boys from South Carolina received these gifts graciously and enthusiastically presented the people souvenirs in return.

The trip produced some fond memories for Kirkland and his friends. In one of his first letters home, Richard shared his experiences with his brother Jesse. The letter was filled with excitement and curiosity. Richard told his brother about the days at Morris Island and the trip from Charleston to Virginia. It didn't sound like a letter from a boy about to go to war. But Richard expressed uncertainty about what the coming days would bring. He had yet to experience the horrors of war.

Richard's letters showed another side too, that he was homesick, and missed his family very much. Even though Richard was a dedicated volunteer, he sometimes wished he could be back with his family on the peaceful farms of Kershaw County. He had never been away from his family for such a long time. He wrote letter after letter and begged for a reply.

Richmond, Virginia
April 28, 1861

Dear Brother,
I write you a few lines to inform you of my location at present. I have been away from home ever since the 8th instant. Everyone in the company has heard from home except me. I have written at least one-half dozen letters and have not received any answer yet.
We were received with a warm reception everywhere. It appeared like there never were such men in the world as South Carolinians.

There is no way to get away from the Virginians for they come regularly to the garrison and every evening to the Cemetery which is in front of the garrison. What is better than all -- they are ladies that mostly call on us!

When we came through Wilmington and Petersburg, we could not turn for the girls wanting Palmettos which we had twisted into cockades pinned to our caps, for which we received bouquets of flowers.

I do not know exactly what the President intends doing with us; yet I understand that we will march to Washington when we leave here. If we do, we will have to go to work for there is no battery to protect us at Washington.

All the public buildings are undermined so as to blow them up as soon as the Yankees find they cannot hold them. Old Abe has a lot of troops in Washington but a third of what he called for.

There are, in Virginia, 70 or 80 thousand troops known and they are still coming in. If it is required, there will be 200 thousand here in a few days.

Nothing more at present, but I remain your affectionate brother.

R.R. Kirkland

Give my love to all the family. Tell them all to write soon. Direct to Captain Kennedy, 2nd Regiment, South Carolina Volunteers, Richmond, Virginia.

Richard Kirkland arrived in Virginia about April 24th, and again answered the roll call -- present for duty. The friendly treatment in Virginia was the same as it had been during the trip North from Charleston. Life in the soldier camps was better than it would be later. The jubilant mood continued. Almost every night, the ladies from the local towns would come to the camps and visit the soldiers there. To Kirkland and his friends, it was the most pleasant side of soldier life. It took away some of the heartache of being away from home and family.

Despite the initial novelty and jubilation soldiering brought to the boys, the adjustment to military life was still tough. Living conditions were not what the young men had grown up with. For the first time, many of the young boys were in the presence of strangers, and far more people than they had previously come in contact with. The physical demands were hard to get used to in Virginia, just as when the Citadel cadets had come to drill the young, novice soldiers.

Being in the army required a discipline most of the Southern boys were not accustomed to. The discipline of daily military life contrasted with the jovial evenings when the ladies from town came to visit. But Richard Kirkland adjusted well. When he wrote letters home to his family, young Kirkland never complained about the discipline, or sharing meals, sleeping quarters, and just about everything else with all the other young boys who had come to fight for the Confederacy.

It didn't take long for the young soldiers to grow impatient while waiting to fight. When the orders came down, sending the men into battle, jubilation filled the camp. The fear that gripped most of the young men remained deep inside them. For every soldier in the regiment, there was a different feeling. But for the most part, the feeling was excitement at finally facing the North and fighting for the cause of freedom, which the young Confederates felt was their cause. However, they wouldn't march to Washington, as Richard had written in his letter. Instead, the Federal troops from Washington intended to march to Richmond, the Confederate capital. Kirkland and the other soldiers would defend Richmond from invading troops.

The festive mood did soon change. And it would only take a few weeks for the realities of war set in. In July, 1861, Kirkland's unit was thrust into combat during the war's first major battle. At Manassas Junction, they encountered a large Federal army determined to march to Richmond and control the Confederate capital. Like the Southern armies, the Federals wanted to put a quick end to the war. The Union intended to defeat the new Confederate States of America, stop its rebellion and bring the country back together. That would happen, but it would take four years and the lives of thousands of Americans.

In its first taste of war, the Second South Carolina Regiment, commanded by Colonel Kershaw, was ordered into battle on July 21st. They marched to face an enemy they knew very little about. All they really knew about the Union army they faced was that the soldiers on the other side were young men fighting for a cause also. The warriors from the South were greeted by fierce rifle and cannon fire from their Union brothers on the opposing lines. Kershaw's young, inexperienced regiment of fighters passed through woods and fields, and marched down unfamiliar roads in pursuit of their enemy. Several times, Kirkland and his comrades were forced to lie flat in the fields to avoid the shower of bullets flying through the air in both directions.

Kershaw's Regiment quickly became an important part of the Confederacy's early defense of Virginia. During the heat of the battle, Private Kirkland and his fellow soldiers crossed a murky creek called Bull Run at a place called Mitchell's Ford. Some of the Southern soldiers crossed the creek on a stone bridge, while others waded across the shallow water. The challengers were waiting for Kirkland's unit on a hill about a half mile away. But the brave, determined South

Carolinians charged up a steep bank, assaulted and smashed a Union line of defense.

The Confederates pushed back the Union army with a spirited charge and unleashed the piercing Rebel yell that would become a well-known Civil War call and a trademark of the Southern zeal. When the Confederates charged into battle, they always screamed that piercing yell while they raced to face the enemy. It was this enthusiasm and fearlessness that led the Southern armies to victory after victory in the first two years of the war. The Confederate soldiers and their generals quickly began to feel like they could never be beaten.

During the violent clash around a place called the Henry House Hill, Kershaw's men fought right in the middle of a furious artillery battle. The fighting around the Henry House was where Confederate General Thomas J. Jackson got his nickname "Stonewall." It was another South Carolina General, Barnard E. Bee, who gave General Jackson the nickname. General Bee reached a hill and saw Jackson standing bravely in front of his troops. Bee shouted, "Look! There stands Jackson like a stone wall. Rally behind the Virginians!" The nickname lived on. The South Carolina troops did rally with the other Confederates, drove the Union soldiers back and claimed the first major victory in the war.

Richard Kirkland and the other men under Colonel Kershaw were a big part of the victory at Bull Run. Bull Run Creek at Manassas Junction was Richard Kirkland's first taste of war, and he fought bravely. Like other young boys of the Confederacy, Richard believed that he and his colleagues would march into Washington and pound President Lincoln's troops. The Southerners thought the war would be short, and that Lincoln and the United States would pull back and allow the Confederate States of America to live among themselves. Many times, the soldiers, generals and politicians from the North and South would be wrong about the war.

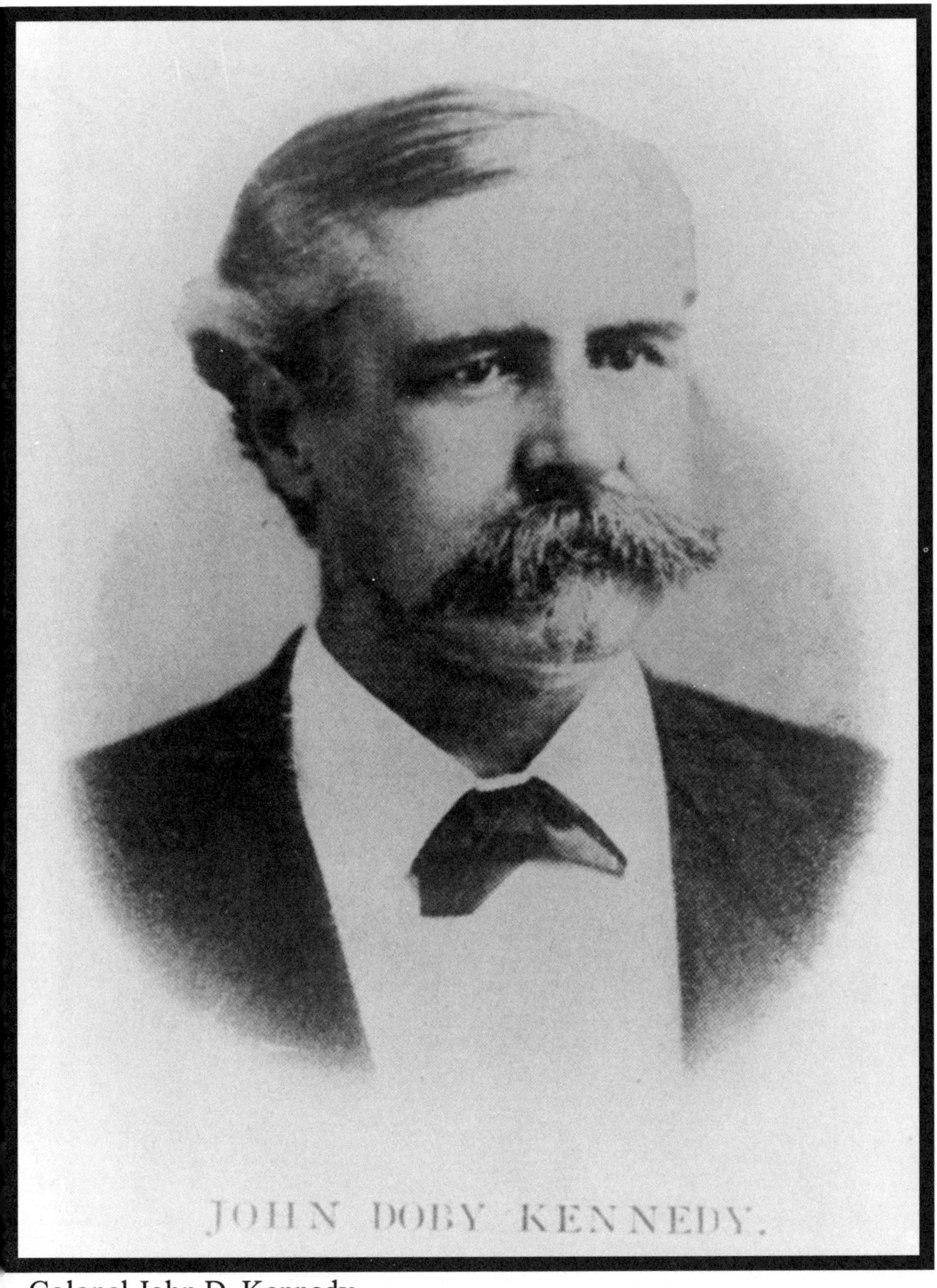
JOHN DOBY KENNEDY.

Camden Archives and Museum

Colonel John D. Kennedy

General Joseph B. Kershaw

*Again and again a new line forms
And the gallant charge is made,
And again and again they fall like grain
In the sweep of the reaper's blade.*

Richard Kirkland fought in all the major battles in Virginia for the next year. In the summer of 1862, after more than fifteen months at war, he was promoted to the rank of sergeant. The promotion was a fitting birthday present as it came right about the time of his 19th birthday. The wearing of sergeant's stripes carried with it more responsibility than just being a sharpshooter infantry private.

Like an astute sergeant, he set a good example for the other troops. He fought to exhaustion at the Seven Days' Battles when the Union army again threatened to march into Richmond. Many of his companions fell dead or wounded. With great care and pain, he wrote home to friends and family with the bad news. He had the unpleasant task of writing to his sister-in-law Rosa, who was married to Richard's older brother, Jesse. Sadly, Richard sent Rosa the bad news of the horrible death of her beloved younger brother Billy Truesdel.

Camp near Richmond
July 4, 1862

Dear Rosa,

    I take this opportunity of writing you all the information that I have in regard to the fight here. I arrived on the line of battle on Thursday after the fighting commenced on Wednesday was a week ago; and not knowing where my regiment was, I borrowed a horse not engaged. I remained on the field until the battle was over for the day, then returned to the camp and went in search of our regiment. I found them about two hours by the sun Friday evening.

    William T. went back with me to the camp of the Kirkwood Rangers and we took supper with Billy and Dan. Then we returned to our regiment.

    The next morning we were sent out on picket. We were up all Saturday night. Early in the morning Sunday we commenced an advance on the enemy. We had several skirmishes through the day but did not engage the enemy until about an hour and a half by the sun. We fought them until 8 or 9 o'clock in the night.

    William, your brother, was killed early in the action by a ball through the head. David Stover, B. Truesdel and Roberson were also killed. When I wrote to Pa, I stated that B. Truesdel was wounded but I found out that his wound was mortal...

    I was completely exhausted when the fight was over. I applied for permission to return to camp and it was granted. I borrowed Dan's horse to ride and rode to

Richmond Monday evening to telegraph Pa. When you write, please let me know if Pa received.

Tuesday evening our regiment was engaged again...I was not with the regiment in the last fight but I'm even with them yet, for I was in the fight on Thursday and they were not.

We have driven the enemy back about twenty miles, captured a great many prisoners and government stores. We are still pursuing. They are under cover of their gunboats and it is impossible to attack them now. They are going down the James River. It is supposed that they are going off on their gunboats. If so, we will not get to whip them any more just now. A Yankee prisoner whom we captured on Sunday says that McClellan made a speech to them on Saturday night and told them that he had been deceived by them and that he would do the best he could for them; that he would take them to the North if he could.

Lt. Benton gave out on the march down and is now in Richmond. I expect to go to Richmond today and will see Benton if I can find him. Lt. J. D. Dunlap is sending me to Richmond to see how our wounded are getting along. I will come to a close by saying that all is well with me at present.

Yours ever the same,

R. R. Kirkland

In his next letter to Rosa, Richard provided details of young Billy's death to help Rosa answer some questions that had troubled her. She had been very sad in her reply to Richard's last letter. It was bad enough that her brother was dead, but the information sent to Rosa was sketchy and agonizing. Richard replied to her letter with frightening detail about her brother's death, hoping to ease her mind, if even just a little. He also tried to put the death of young Billy into some kind of religious perspective. Richard was a deeply religious man and even from the battlefield he wrote sincere, supportive letters to try and ease the pain that the people back home felt. His follow-up letter to Rosa was written on captured stationery. Even though it cleared up questions about Billy's death, it graphically detailed the horrors of war, and the terrible way young people suffered during the war.

Richard's letter also had some good news. He was always excited to write his father, brothers and sister back at Flat Rock about the time he was able to spend with his brothers Dan, Billy and Sam. Between battles during the Summer of 1862, he sometimes went to the camp of the Kirkwood Rangers, where his brothers Dan and Billy served. Before the brothers went out on pickets -- guard duty -- they ate supper together and shared some home-made cakes that had been sent to them from their family back home. Richard wrote home about these meetings in memorable detail.

Camp McLaws, Virginia
July 24, 1862

Dear Rosa,
I received yours of the 11th on yesterday and I take this opportunity to respond. This leaves us all well. I am sorry to see you write so sad. William has done only what we will all have to soon do. It's time we

communicate...the loss of one so kind and just; one whom we loved and esteemed. But we must recollect that it is not our will but HIS that must be done.

You seem to think that he might have been saved if anyone of his friends could have been present to assist him. That, alas, is not so. The accursed ball had done its work. It passed through his teeth and into his neck which killed him instantly.

You requested me to let you know if William and Sam ever had the opportunity of eating any of the cakes you sent them. They did not. William and I went up to the camp of the Kirkwood Rangers the evening before we went out on picket. We took supper with Dan and Billy and had some cake for supper, but it was out of Dan's box. Our box was not opened. Before we could get back, all of the cakes of our box were spoiled except a few which were left with Dan until we moved back to our present camps and then Sam and William were both absent. Therefore you see that neither boy nor I received any benefit from our box.

We have no news of any importance from the enemy. We have commenced to destroy the Yankee breastworks on the Chickahominy River this morning.

I have not heard from Sam since he left. He has gone home to Flat Rock...

I will close and request you to write soon as it takes a letter about two weeks to reach us now.

Yours V.
R.R. Kirkland

Camp life gave the soldiers a lot of time to write letters. In fact, when they weren't fighting or marching, writing letters was one of the most popular ways for the young soldiers to pass the time. But there was always plenty of entertainment -- music, simple games of sport, and even cockfights. The games and letter-writing usually had to wait until the chores were done. There was always wood to chop and clothes to mend. Many of the soldiers took pride in being able to sew their worn clothing as skillfully as the women back home.

Living quarters in the camp were very humble, much different from the spacious, warm plantation house where Richard Kirkland grew up. During the summer months, soldiers slept in tents. There were different kinds -- some large and some small. But they were always very crowded. One popular tent was the Sibley, which was named after the man who invented it. It was cone-shaped, and looked similar to an Indian teepee. Even though the tent was fairly large, it became very cozy when twelve to twenty men slept in it, with their feet to the center of the tent. Sometimes soldiers were packed so tightly that they could not roll over. When one man shifted, they all had to shift.

The summers were miserably hot, and the winters dangerously cold. During the first long winter, Richard Kirkland sometimes had to share one blanket with his pal T. M. Rembert. They were as close as two friends could be, more like brothers. They fought side by side for many months and through some of the war's greatest battles. Rembert was with Richard at Fredericksburg and an eyewitness to Kirkland's marvelous, merciful act. But their friendship would be tragically cut short at the fateful battle of Chickamauga.

In the winter, most of the men stayed in log huts. The officer quarters were usually warm and spacious. But enlisted men were still packed tightly in the small houses, built with logs and packed with mud and clay. The lucky soldiers had stoves to keep them warm in winter.

A great deal of work went into building the log houses. Cutting timber and chopping logs was a never-ending job. Sometimes whole areas of woodlands would be stripped bare by the army constructing houses for the winter. But there was always plenty of mud and clay. A good rainstorm or melting snow turned a soldier's camp into a mud hole. It never seemed to dry out.

The men of Kershaw struggled through that first winter like everyone else. By the Summer of 1862, Kershaw was elevated to the rank of brigadier general and given command of what became known as Kershaw's Brigade. John D. Kennedy was promoted to colonel to take command of the Second South Carolina Regiment, in Kershaw's Brigade. During the Summer of 1962, Richard Kirkland transferred from Company E, Second Regiment, South Carolina Volunteers, to Company G, the Flat Rock Guards, so he could fight alongside his friends and neighbors.

In battle, or between the skirmishes, Sergeant Kirkland distinguished himself by his courage and compassion. After the Seven Days' Battles in 1862, he was sent to Richmond to check on the wounded men of his company and reported back to his lieutenant on their condition. He was often given responsibilities of great importance in his company, and whether the job was large or small, Richard Kirkland gave it his best effort.

At the end of the Summer of that same year, Kirkland and his comrades crossed into Maryland for the first time. They now became the invading force. Instead of defending Virginia and the Confederacy, they became the aggressors in taking the war into Union country. General Lee sent his worn, but determined army into Maryland and charged the Federal defenders at Harper's Ferry and Sharpsburg. The Antietam Campaign, as these battles were called, would last about a week in September of 1862, the major battle taking place on the 17th and 18th.

But the men of General Kershaw had to fight several days before that just to get into the position where Lee wanted them. As they marched through the hills, Kirkland's Second South Carolina Regiment encountered the enemy pickets, and skirmishes broke out before the enemy withdrew its pickets. Kershaw's men, with the help of a Mississippi unit, drove the enemy out of the area of Elk Ridge, which overlooked Harper's Ferry. Kershaw's Brigade then continued its march. At about six o'clock in the evening on the 12th, they reached another Federal line of defense. General Kershaw put his brigade in two lines, extending across the summit of Elk Ridge, with Richard Kirkland and the Second Regiment in the rear of the formation. They camped for the night there, but slept with their rifles by their side in preparation for the next day's fight.

The next morning, Kershaw's Brigade engaged 1,200 diligent Union troops in the hills and mountains known as the Maryland Heights. It was a fierce attack with the two armies only about a hundred yards apart during most of the fighting. Losses were heavy on both sides and Kershaw was forced to bring up his reserve units to join the fight. At every turn, the Confederate troops were stoutly resisted by zealous Union soldiers. Richard Kirkland and his pals fought bravely and Kirkland came out of the battle unhurt.

In the late morning, a regiment of Barksdale's Mississippi brigade came up on the Federal forces from behind, resulting in the Northerners being almost surrounded. The men of General Barksdale then fired into the rear of the Federal lines and the Union army retreated quickly, escaping down the side of the mountain. Kershaw's men captured prisoners and guns during the enemy retreat and the general left Barksdale's men to occupy the point of the mountain.

Kershaw's men were then able to move on and get into position near Sharpsburg. Arriving in Sharpsburg on Wednesday, September 17, 1862, they were exhausted, but immediately ordered to support the Confederate troops already positioned there. The Second Regiment was commanded to march double-quick into position in deep woods. Before they could get properly organized, the enemy started firing on them fiercely. The Second Regiment was the first of Kershaw's commands to engage the enemy on this day. Kirkland and his comrades turned to face their opponents, who stood in strong numbers no more than sixty yards away.

The gallant Confederate warriors fought so vigorously that the Federal army turned and retreated, with the Second Regiment in hot pursuit. Despite the success of this movement, Colonel Kennedy was painfully wounded during the battle at Sharpsburg. He tried to fight on, but General Kershaw ordered him from the field. Kennedy's courage and bravery was just one example of the gallant conduct of Kershaw's troops that day.

In his report to Major General McLaws, the division commander, Kershaw offered this statement about the soldiers of his command:

> *The acts of individual heroism performed on this memorable day are so numerous that regimental commanders have not attempted to particularize them...*
>
> *I cannot too highly commend to your notice the gallant conduct of the troops of my command...*
>
> *J.B. Kershaw*
> *Brigadier-General*

The Antietam Campaign was not the convincing victory General Lee had hoped for. Nor was it a defeat. It was one of several attempts by General Lee and the Southern army to take the war into the Northern states. When it was apparent nothing more could be accomplished in Maryland, Lee ordered Kershaw's Brigade and the rest of the units back into Virginia.

Eventually, the army of General Lee and the men of Kershaw's Brigade were able to cross back into Virginia safely. They then began the long and exhausting march to Fredericksburg, camping several times along the way. The tired army moved into the long winter that was just over the horizon. Only victories would ease the sting of the cold season. Fredericksburg would provide that victory, and much more.

And then from out of the battle smoke
There falls on the lead-swept air
From the whitening lips that are ready to die
The piteous moan and the plaintive cry
For "water" everywhere.

To the Confederate soldiers and generals, it was not surprising that the South was winning the war. Despite being outnumbered in men and weapons, the South's superb leadership and determination turned close battles into Southern victories. On Virginia soil, the Confederate soldiers fought with all their heart and soul, and refused to allow the Union army to seize the upper hand.

Richard Kirkland's conduct in battle was earning him the reputation of a strong, stalwart soldier. But it was at the Battle of Fredericksburg where Richard displayed the enormous courage and nobility that prompts people today to honor and remember him. He was always a strong-willed, fearless Confederate soldier. But that was common in Kershaw's Brigade and in the entire Army of Northern Virginia. In front of the Union and Confederate armies at Fredericksburg, Richard Kirkland changed from an ordinary soldier to an extraordinary leader.

Fredericksburg was strategically important, astride the vital route that connected Richmond and Washington. It had to be defended. The Confederates could not allow the Union army to control the road to the Southern capital.

The Federal troops actually had a grand opportunity to easily capture Fredericksburg, and move on toward Richmond. They marched ahead of their enemy and reached the outskirts of Fredericksburg before the Southerners. Before the Confederates had built their strong defense in the hills and fields around Fredericksburg, thousands of Union soldiers were camped just across the river. But the Union army could not cross the frigid Rappahannock River without the equipment needed to build pontoon bridges. They had to wait while only a small Confederate force guarded Fredericksburg.

To the good fortune of the Southern army, the necessary Union supplies took several weeks to arrive. Union President Abraham Lincoln and his generals were angry and impatient, anxious to win a decisive victory against General Robert E. Lee on Virginia soil. But the Union leaders were helpless against the icy waters of the river.

The Army of the Potomac, the United States forces, were in disarray and desperate for a victory. Morale was low in the camps. Their generals were being badly criticized by politicians and by many of the blue-clad Union soldiers. Just days before the Union army marched to Fredericksburg, Lincoln replaced General McClellan with General Ambrose Burnside, who accepted the command of the Federal army with reluctance. He felt incapable of leading the army, and knew he was taking command when the Union army was discouraged and defeated. General Burnside also felt relentless pressure to deliver a quick, decisive strike to prove his worth to President Lincoln.

The delay in getting the bridges across the river put Burnside at a disadvantage from which he would never recover. The pressure to win and send good news back to President Lincoln forced General

Burnside into making decisions that needlessly sent many good men to their deaths.

The costly delay gave General Robert E. Lee the time he needed to bring in more troops and strengthen his position. The Confederate men continued to dig in while the Federals waited. Soon, the Southern armies formed a strong line of defense, entrenched behind fences and walls, on roads and on the crest of small hills.

Finally, the equipment arrived and the bridges across the river were constructed. On the cold morning of December 13, 1862, General Ambrose Burnside sent his troops across the cold Rappahannock. The Southern boys waited on the other side. They were content to give up the town to the Union army and hold onto their strong defense at the rear of the town. The Union soldiers would be forced to charge uphill across open fields to reach them.

The brigade of General Kershaw, which included Richard Kirkland and the Second South Carolina Regiment, took up its position at the foot of Lee's Hill near a small creek called Hazel Run. On the extreme right flank of the Confederate line, the divisions were commanded by General Stonewall Jackson. It was in front of Jackson's men where the Federal army made its first attack. Some of the most severe action in the early stages of the battle took place on this flank of the Confederate line. Burnside's men forced several small breaks in the Confederate right flank, but the men of General Stonewall Jackson held back the main thrust. When the first charge failed, Burnside decided to push hard against other sections of the solid Confederate line.

After crossing the river, the Federal sharpshooters in the town of Fredericksburg fought from the protection of homes and other buildings in the town. But they could do no harm to the Confederate lines. On Burnside's order, Union soldiers abandoned the protection of the village and moved into open fields to charge the Southerners, who waited patiently in their fortified defensive posts. It was cold, and the

Federal soldiers and generals grew impatient. General Lee's men fought from their positions, and were happy to stay in their strong lines and await the Union soldiers. The blue-clad Federals had an impossible task, to break the hardened lines of the Confederates. Burnside ordered his men to leave the town and charge up the hills where the Confederates were fortified and strong.

Around midday, Burnside began to concentrate his attack on the middle of the Confederate defense, at a place called Marye's Heights, where General James Longstreet, a native of South Carolina, was in command. Unfortunately for the Federal forces, the Confederate defense was strongest there.

General Lee had fortified the area of Marye's Heights with more than 2,500 brave Georgians under the command of General Thomas R. R. Cobb. His determined soldiers were positioned four-deep on Telegraph Road, which was also referred to as Sunken Road. The Sunken Road was a main route from Fredericksburg to Spotsylvania Court House, and the wheels from the horse-drawn wagons had packed the muddy earth tight, until it was lower than the edges of the road. The people of Fredericksburg had then built a sturdy, stone wall to protect the wagons from toppling off the road and down the slopes below. The Sunken Road provided a splendid fighting position for the Confederates.

The soldiers were well protected by a shoulder-high stone wall. Brave men crowded onto the muddy Sunken Road and waited for the Union charge. Behind them, the road was bordered by a wooded hill that led up to a fine country estate called the Marye's House. General Lee could not have asked for a better place to build a strong defense. The Union advance would be uphill and across open fields. Southern boys loaded their rifles, sat behind the wall, or stood in a trench that had been dug on the edge of the road. Some fired at snipers in the town and behind the houses and barns below. But many others just waited, leaning on their muskets, waiting for the Union army to charge.

The first Union assault on Marye's Heights came in the freezing late morning. It was halted by the Southerners with a steady barrage of rifle fire. By firing in shifts, they poured a steady volley of fire on the poor Union soldiers who stumbled in wave after wave up the slope. It only took a few minutes for the bodies of dead and wounded Union soldiers to start piling up on the hill below the Sunken Road. But none of the charging Union soldiers could help their fallen comrades. They were much too vulnerable to the barrage of bullets streaming from the rifles of the Confederate infantrymen.

The men of Kershaw's Brigade engaged the enemy and defended their line about two hundred yards from the stone wall at the foot of Lee's Hill. They were also well fortified. The Union charge in their front was not as strong as the Union spearhead at the stone wall. Kershaw's men fought bravely and held back the challengers. Just before one o'clock in the afternoon, General Kershaw was ordered to move two of his regiments down to the Sunken Road to support the men fighting there. Marye's Heights had become the center of the Battle of Fredericksburg, and the Union assault there continued to intensify. Kershaw's first task was to bring more ammunition to the gallant Georgians battling the Union charge. Kershaw's men were fighters too, and they would soon join their brothers from Cobb's brigade in holding back the relentless charge of their Union enemy.

The first South Carolina regiment to move to their new position at Marye's Heights was the Third Regiment. The men came under heavy fire as they left their position and marched down Telegraph Road. Many good soldiers of the South Carolina Third Regiment fell. But like all the great South Carolina regiments, the Third quickened its pace, and General Kershaw pushed them on. Below Lee's Hill, and down the Telegraph Road, officers barked out instructions in the middle of the intense Union fire.

"Move out!" commanders yelled.

"Cover the advance!"

The companies of Richard Kirkland's Second South Carolina Regiment were ordered to intensify their fire on the enemy and cover the transfer of the Third Regiment. Kirkland and many of his friends exposed themselves to heavy Union rifle fire near Hazel Run to protect the movement of their brothers of the Third Regiment. Later, after the long battle ended, they were commended for their brave fighting while covering the Third Regiment's march. Their job of protecting the Third Regiment didn't last long. Only minutes later, the Second South Carolina Regiment received directions to move out. They left their protected positions quickly and marched fearlessly down Telegraph Road to the stone wall.

While the South Carolina reinforcements were advancing to the Sunken Road, General Cobb was mortally wounded and taken to a small field hospital behind Marye's Heights, where he died of his wounds. General McLaws, division commander in General Longstreet's Corps, ordered Kershaw to ride to Marye's Heights and take command of the men fighting there. Kershaw ordered the rest of his brigade to advance quickly to Marye's Heights, then boldly rode on horseback into the intense fighting at Marye's Heights, urging his men to move swiftly. His ride was applauded by the other generals as an act of extreme bravery.

"Hold the line!" he called to the Georgians fighting at the stone wall. "Reinforcements are coming!" His superiors had told him to keep possession of their stronghold at the stone wall at all costs. And knowing that, he shouted motivation to the troops now under his command, both from South Carolina and Georgia. After leading the repositioning of his men, he arrived at the Stevens House to take up his new headquarters. The Stevens House was built against the stone wall on the edge of the battlefield. From the second-floor window, General Kershaw had a wide-open and rather treacherous view of the battle on the slopes below.

Kershaw ordered his Third Regiment and Seventh Regiment to take up the line near the Marye's House on the hill. The rest of his brigade, including Richard Kirkland's Second Regiment, were placed on the Sunken Road in support of the men from Georgia still fighting fearlessly there. The Second Regiment was still commanded by Kirkland's friend from Kershaw County, Colonel Kennedy, who had recovered and returned to duty.

Richard Kirkland and the other men of Kershaw's Brigade supported Cobb's men all day on the 13th of December. Several thousand men were now jammed behind the stone wall on the muddy Sunken Road. The fighting was fierce and never-ending. Kirkland and his friends fired in shifts all afternoon. When they looked over the wall to aim their weapons, they looked directly into the charge of thousands of determined and fearless Union soldiers. Behind the wall, one row of Southern riflemen would stand at the wall and fire, then step back to reload their weapons. Then another group of Confederate soldiers would fire, step back and reload. A third and fourth line fired, one after another. Then the first group would step forward again, struggling through the mass of soldiers, and trying to maintain their footing on the frozen, slick road. With great effort, the Confederate soldiers were able to fire continuously. But each time they stood up, the Confederates exposed themselves to artillery fire and the swarms of bullets being fired from Union snipers and the advancing troops.

The Union soldiers continued to charge the wall all day and sustained terrific casualties during their bloody assault on Marye's Heights. Some of the blue-clad Northern soldiers came within ten yards of the wall before the bullets of the Confederates stopped them. But not one Union soldier reached the wall.

General Kershaw observed the battle from his new headquarters at the Stevens House. He sent members of his staff to keep the other generals posted on the progress of the battle. At one point, he sent his aide, Captain Doby, to ride along the Sunken Road and motivate the men fighting there. Doby exhorted the Georgia and South Carolina troops to fight bravely.

"You must hold your positions at all hazards!" Doby yelled to the men. "We must not give up this good ground!"

Burnside's men made nearly a dozen bloody, desperate charges at the stone wall below Marye's Heights. But late in the afternoon, as the bitter cold of night began to fall, the charges stopped and the rifle fire slowed. The sharpshooters on both sides continued to pick out enemy targets, but most of the fighting stopped. Both armies were exhausted. The Federal units who had been assigned to charge the stone wall were devastated. The thick smoke from the daylong battle mixed with the fog to form a gray, gloomy cloud over the battlefield.

The Union soldiers held their positions back in the town, but couldn't rescue the thousands of their dead and wounded lying in agony on the slope below Marye's Heights. Union men unhurt on the hill stayed down, using the dead bodies of their comrades for protection. The Confederate soldiers rested behind the stone wall but remained alert. Even exposing their head above the wall invited a volley of bullets from the Union snipers.

A dark mood fell on the battlefield with the night. The Confederate soldiers sat or lay crammed behind the stone wall, desperate to stay warm and alert to movements of the enemy. Just yards in front of them, on the frozen plain, nine or ten thousand Federal soldiers lay dead and wounded. The injured Union boys were helpless and cold, in terrible pain and unable to get back to their lines. Their fellow soldiers could not come forward to help them without being shot by the Confederates still armed and ready behind the stone wall. The men on both sides could only wait.

Night fell and the agonizing cries for water and warmth filled the air. Out on the frozen field, Union soldiers were forced to strip the clothes and coats from their dead comrades to stay warm. In a most desperate act, one Union colonel, Joshua Lawrence Chamberlain, piled the dead bodies of his own men all around him to stay warm and shield him from the bullets of the Confederate sharpshooters. He could not sleep the whole night. These were his men. But he wanted to stay alive, wanted to live to fight another day for his beloved Union. During the night, he crawled to some of his men and tried to comfort them or give them water.

He didn't know Richard Kirkland, nor did Kirkland know Chamberlain. They would never meet. They were enemies in battle, but shared some of the same attributes of compassion and courage. Chamberlain would rise to fame seven months later at Gettysburg. Richard Kirkland would carve his name into history in just hours. Neither would realize just how close they would come to each other, on the hill at Marye's Heights or at Gettysburg the following summer. But on this night, they were two men, on opposite sides, fighting for what they believed was right and just.

Richard Kirkland stayed at his post throughout the night. He and his comrades from Georgia and South Carolina were forced to endure the sounds of pain and fear. All night long the cries of wounded Union soldiers scorched the ears of the nearby Confederates. The dark from the night and the cloud of smoke and frost obscured the view of the icy slope. But the sounds that came from the field clearly illustrated the scene of pain and death.

The night was long. It was a cold, horrible night for both armies. Even though the dying men were the enemy, it wasn't easy for any of the Confederate soldiers to endure the terrible sounds of pain and death that lasted all night. Richard Kirkland sat close to his friend T.M. Rembert and listened to the desperation and agony of the Union cries. These men were his brothers, even though they were enemies on the other side of the wall. Their screams pierced his soul. He couldn't rest when the calls for help were so close and desperate.

As morning slowly approached, the soldiers on both sides expected the fighting to continue. General Burnside of the Union army was set to make another desperate charge at Marye's Heights. He felt that he had to break the lines and send a message of victory back to President Lincoln. But his fellow generals urged him not to attack again, so the Union army continued to occupy the town of Fredericksburg but did not attack. The Confederates held fast to their defensive positions on the hills above the town. Kershaw kept his men alert and ready to defend their positions. He had just won a great victory. He would not relax and let the Federal troops catch his regiments unprepared.

The dreadful cries of the wounded Union soldiers continued throughout the morning. The lingering fog and smoke kept the battlefield dark and obscure. But the cries still found their way out of the fog. Richard Kirkland listened with a heavy heart. Finally, neither his heart nor his ears could stand it any longer. He had not slept all night. The smoke from the previous day's battle still choked his burning lungs. But the cries from the battlefield troubled him more.

Colonel Joshua Lawrence Chamberlain

Sergeant Kirkland makes his daring plea to General Kershaw.

And into the presence of Kershaw brave
There comes a fair-faced lad
With quivering lips as his cap he tips
'I can't stand this,' he said.

The night had been cold and long, so cold that razor-thin ice shavings had formed on the beards of the soldiers from the North and the South. Even though the men on the other side of the stone wall were Sergeant Kirkland's enemies in battle, they were brave men just the same. They were Americans, just like Kirkland, who were on the other side of a great conflict. He had listened helplessly to their unanswered cries for hours. In his heart, he wanted to jump over the wall right then and try to relieve their suffering in any way possible. That's just the type of man he was. But Richard Kirkland was also a soldier who would never abandon his post without permission. He knew there was nothing he could do to help the dying Union soldiers without being granted leave by his superiors. Finally, he couldn't listen any longer. He had to do something, anything to help ease their suffering.

The mid-morning fog was burning off slowly. The Union troops were still in position to attack, but didn't seem able to strike again. Kirkland had sat behind the wall long enough! He had to act.

Finally, Richard sought out the captain of his company and made a strange, daring and unbelievable request. To the shock of the young officer in charge of Kirkland's company, the soldier came to him seeking permission to leap over the wall and into the teeth of danger, for the simple purpose of offering water to the poor enemy soldiers. The captain hesitated, but only for an instant. The decision was an easy one for him to make. He could not possibly accept the responsibility for allowing Kirkland to attempt such a daring act. A court martial would certainly follow if the young captain allowed such a dangerous, outrageous request. So the company commander sent Richard to see the regimental commander, Colonel John D. Kennedy. Colonel Kennedy had known Richard Kirkland for many years. If anyone knew the kind of young man Richard Kirkland was, it was Kennedy. But he too was stunned by such an extraordinary proposal. Kennedy must have thought about what the people back home would think when they learned that he had let Kirkland roam into the middle of a fierce, volatile battlefield. Kennedy would not grant the approval Richard Kirkland sought. But he couldn't deny such a brave offer either. So Kennedy reluctantly authorized Kirkland to report directly to General Kershaw to make the request.

Young Kirkland could have changed his mind at this point. No one would have ever questioned his bravery if Richard had withdrawn his strange request. In fact, the men would have thought him wise to reconsider. But no one successfully talked him out of attempting this daring act he was so determined to perform. He made no attempt to withdraw his proposal.

Undaunted, Sergeant Kirkland went to Kershaw's headquarters at the Stevens House to ask permission of the general whom he respected very much. Perhaps that respect made it easier for him to approach the general. Perhaps that respect made it more difficult for Kirkland to place such a notorious plea before Kershaw. Kirkland didn't want to trouble Kershaw, especially at a time when so many important decisions faced the general. But the young sergeant had made up his mind, and his general's approval meant everything.

Sergeant Richard Kirkland was seeking approval to perform a daring, suicidal act of compassion. Frequently he had risked his life in the perils of battle. But to risk life needlessly didn't seem practical for any young man. He was still a teenager at nineteen years old, but also a weathered veteran of a half dozen major battles. He never hesitated, once he had determined in his mind the action he had to take.

General Kershaw certainly did not expect his visitor. His mind was fully absorbed in the battle which had taken place just the day before. He needed to know every detail of the battle. He wanted to know more than anything the intentions of the opposing generals just across the river.

From a room on the top floor of the house, Kershaw surveyed the battlefield where 30,000 Union troops had attempted to storm his lines. About a third of those Union troops lay cold and restless on the frozen field below. Kershaw was proud of the great victory his men had achieved, but he was troubled by what he saw. The scene tore at his heart. After staring at the pitiful scene in front of him, Kershaw was perhaps better prepared for the approach of Richard Kirkland. There is no reasonable explanation why a general would allow one of his men to attempt such a valiant stunt in the heat of battle. But Kirkland's request would defy all reason. It was a request from the heart and inner soul.

Aides came in and out of the headquarters. Orders and reports were being delivered at every turn. Every officer had his mind on the battle -- what the Union troops would do next. How would the Confederate army respond? General Kershaw continued to stare out the window. A victory was already achieved for General Lee and the Confederacy. What lay ahead, he could not even imagine, but he could not stand to leave the window and his constant watch, even though he exposed himself to the Union sharpshooters down the hill near Fredericksburg.

Kirkland's footsteps on the stairs blended in with the rest of the noise in the house. Then, the knock came, and Kirkland was granted permission to enter the general's private office. The first thing Kershaw noticed about young Kirkland was the demonstrative expression on his face. The sergeant's determination was apparent immediately. Kershaw was accustomed to receiving captains and majors, officers with orders from ranking generals and reports from the battle.

General Kershaw was totally unprepared for this guest, and Kirkland didn't keep the general in suspense. He came directly to the point and spoke boldly to his great commander. Kirkland's heart raced as he stood firmly in front of Kershaw and let his feelings out.

"General, I can't stand this!" Kirkland was as fearless before his general as he would be minutes later in front of the Union sharpshooters.

"What is the matter, Sergeant Kirkland?" General Kershaw asked.

Young Kirkland reached into his soul for courage. He spoke up again. "All night and all day I have heard these poor men crying for water. And I can stand it no longer. Those poor fellows out there are our enemies, it is true. But they are wounded and dying, and they are helpless. I have come to ask permission to take leave of my post and give them water."

The general's first feelings must have been shock. But profound admiration overtook him.

"Kirkland, don't you see the danger? If you were to place your cap on your ramrod, and elevate it above the wall, it would be riddled with bullets immediately. Don't you know that you would get a bullet through the head the moment you stepped over the wall?"

General Kershaw could have refused Kirkland's request immediately, and sent the young man back to his post. At first, Kershaw did refuse. But, at the same time, the general seemed to plead with his young friend and soldier. Now it was Kershaw who was almost begging, appealing with all his heart for Kirkland to reconsider.

"You will be killed instantly if you attempt such a mission," Kershaw said again.

"Yes sir," Kirkland replied. "I know all about that. But if you will let me, I am willing to try it."

General Kershaw paused again. He must have wished that such a request would have never been made. He didn't want to say yes, but seemed powerless to disapprove such a noble and courageous request. Perhaps with a touch of guilt in his heart, Kershaw issued the permission while still urging Kirkland to withdraw his strange, fearless request.

"Kirkland, I ought not to allow you to run such a risk, but the sentiment which compels you is so noble, and indicates so magnificently what a glorious soldier you are, that I will not refuse your request, trusting that God will protect you. You may go."

Kirkland's eyes erupted with pleasure, but should have been filled with fear. It would take a miracle for the young soldier to return from his mission unharmed. Kershaw must have wondered if he had just sent Kirkland to his death. But the young sergeant showed no signs of the intense terror that should have gripped his heart. He had no thought of turning back, even though Kirkland surely knew himself that he was putting his life in extreme danger.

"Thank you, sir," he said, and ran rapidly down the stairs. In his enthusiasm, he probably even forgot to salute the general when he was dismissed.

The sharp sound of Kirkland's boots pounding down the stairs now could be heard throughout the house. But at the front door, young

Kirkland paused for a brief moment, then turned again and charged back up the stairs.

His footsteps were heard again as he bounded back up the stairs and into Kershaw's room again. The general thought and hoped that perhaps Kirkland had lost his courage. But Kershaw was mistaken. Sergeant Kirkland stood in front of General Kershaw again.

"General, can I show a white handkerchief?" Kirkland asked.

"No, Kirkland, you can't do that," Kershaw said firmly. The general was afraid the display of a white handkerchief might give the Union generals the assumption the Confederates wanted to talk, or even surrender.

"All right, sir," Kirkland said. "I'll take the chance." He charged from the room for the second time, and the smile remained on his face.

From his window, General Kershaw kept a close watch on his sergeant during the entire mission of mercy. He was extremely nervous about the permission he had granted, and could only pray to God that the boy would not be harmed. No one wanted to see Kirkland return safely to his post more than the brigade commander.

If any of Sergeant Kirkland's comrades were aware at first of his mission, none was brave enough to volunteer to help. They made but one contribution. Many of Kirkland's friends donated their canteens to his mission. So, completely alone, Sergeant Kirkland gathered as many canteens as he could carry in both arms, strapping other canteens around his neck. He left his rifle, the one in which he had carved the initials "R.K." He couldn't be bothered with a weapon, but needed his hands free to carry all the canteens he could.

He crawled over the wall to the side of the Stevens House. He filled the canteens at the Stevens well, exposing himself to enemy fire from down the hill, but shielded by the dense smoke and fog which still lingered thick on the battlefield. From the window just above Kirkland's head, General Kershaw watched with anxiety.

Richard Kirkland never hesitated. He knew the peril, but he ignored the danger, knowing that he could be shot dead in an instant. Somehow, he gathered all the courage he could arouse. With no thought for his own life, the young man stepped from the cloud of smoke and fog and into the cold heart of the battlefield. He would return a great man, to be honored by other men, by soldiers from the North and South.

The moment Richard abandoned the protection of the stone wall and the Stevens House, and walked into the battlefield, sharp sounds pierced the air -- the deafening burst of rifle fire from the Union sharpshooters. They assumed Richard Kirkland had gone onto the field to rob the dead and wounded Union soldiers. Kirkland ignored their fire and refused to back down from his mission. He fearlessly pushed on, struggling with his heavy load.

After what must have seemed like a long time, he safely reached the first wounded soldier lying cold and helpless on the frozen plain. Richard knelt beside the enemy brother and gently raised the wounded man's head with the greatest of care, resting it against his own chest. Then he poured the water down the thirsty man's burning throat. Kirkland straightened out the wounded soldier's broken limb and placed a knapsack under his head. Sergeant Kirkland covered the wounded man with an overcoat and left his comrade a full canteen. He took the Union soldier's empty canteen and moved on to the next blue-clad casualty.

The Federal sharpshooters in Fredericksburg soon recognized the mission of their brave adversary, and they laid down their rifles and watched in amazement. Kirkland's action brought a wave of new cries from the helpless men scattered on the cold ground. Blood froze to the beards of the fallen men. From all parts of the field they begged,

"Water, water, for God's sakes, water!" Many of the wounded soldiers were too weak and hurt to speak, but could only raise one trembling hand into the air. Their silent calls were also answered by Sergeant Kirkland. Like an angel from heaven, an incredible Southern boy of nineteen relieved the thirst of the wounded Union soldiers.

When his first supply of canteens ran out, Sergeant Kirkland walked quickly back to the well and filled the canteens a second time. When he left the battlefield and returned to the modest protection of the house and well, shots from both sides rang out again and the battle temporarily continued. But when Kirkland once again appeared on the field, the rifles became silent. His mission of mercy continued.

For almost two hours, he went from man to man, trying to ease their pain and soothe their thirst. He tried to warm their bodies while cooling the fever that scorched their mouth and throat. He went back to the well, filling his canteens many times. The soldiers on both sides watched him intently, amazed at what they saw. Their cheers lifted his spirits and pushed him to press on. The loudest cheers came from the Federal soldiers still pinned at the bottom of the hill.

Sergeant Kirkland didn't rest until every man in the area around him had been taken care of. One dying Union soldier thrust a letter to his family into Richard's cold hands, using his last dying breath to request that Kirkland see that the letter be delivered after his death, which was certain. Another soldier entrusted Kirkland with a watchbox. The dying blue-clad soldier asked Richard to send the box to his girlfriend, but insisted that Richard keep the pocket watch for himself.

When Kirkland's mission of mercy was finished, he vaulted back across the wall without a scratch on him. He slumped behind the protection of the wall, exhausted. Cheers from both armies still filled the air, and perhaps took away, just for a few moments, the agony and gloom that rested on that battlefield.

Richard Kirkland returned to his post and resumed his duty immediately. General Kershaw breathed a great sigh of relief. He would remember for the rest of his life what he had witnessed. Kirkland's young friend, T.M. Rembert, would recall years later the great act of mercy, and record it in his personal diary.

Colonel W. D. Trantham, an officer in Kershaw's Brigade, watched Kirkland's great compassionate act. He would remember forever Kirkland's brave deed and would write about it later. He would also fight on the battlefield when Kirkland fell mortally wounded a year later, and Trantham's stirring account of Richard Kirkland's last charge would be published many times.

But no one had time to celebrate or even pause, especially General Kershaw. When the midday sun had burned off the morning fog, he could see that the enemy was still in position to attack, and he told his men to bravely hold their position. Richard Kirkland again took his rifle in hand and sat behind the wall, prepared for the Union assault that the Confederates felt was sure to come.

General Burnside wanted to make another charge on Marye's Heights. He felt pressure to take the position, even though he knew his men had already been severely beaten. But he wanted to send President Lincoln the message that the Union army had finally succeeded at Fredericksburg.

Fortunately, Burnside's officers pleaded with him not to attack Marye's Heights again, and Burnside finally agreed with them. During the night, the Union commander withdrew his forces back across the river and left Fredericksburg in the hands of Robert E. Lee's army.

Richard Kirkland returned to the ranks, unchanged on the outside. But inside, his life had to be different. He had not only performed an unthinkable act of courage and mercy, but he did it knowing he would probably die. Even knowing the risks, he had been willing to die for the benefit of others, if only to bring them comfort for a brief moment. He truly was an angel of mercy.

On the plains below the blue lines glow
And the bugle rings out clear,
As with bated breath they march to death
And a soldier's honored bier.

Sergeant Kirkland's valor and sympathy at Fredericksburg earned him respect and admiration of soldiers on both sides who witnessed his courageous act. But unfortunately, Kirkland would never receive the recognition he deserved, at least not while he was alive. The well-deserved honor would not come until later, many years after his death. But his daring mission of mercy at Fredericksburg was a topic of conversation among Federal and Confederate troops alike, and he was called the *Angel of Marye's Heights* by people who shared the story of what he had done.

Not only had he been willing to aid soldiers who in war were the enemy, but he had been willing to sacrifice his own life if necessary. And when it was over, just as suddenly as he had decided to act extraordinarily, he became an ordinary soldier again.

Immediately after the Battle of Fredericksburg, Richard was given leave from his company and the horror of the war and sent home to Kershaw County. His assignment was to recruit other young South Carolinians into Kershaw's Brigade, which had built the reputation as a brave, relentless fighting force. But the brigade, like the whole Southern army, was losing men fast, and needed to replace them. It would only be a matter of time before the Union advantage in numbers and resources would overpower the Confederate superiority in leadership and determination.

The fighting spirit of Kershaw's Brigade spread throughout the Confederate army. One company commander of the Second South Carolina Regiment was extremely impressed by the performance of his men at Fredericksburg. The commander, Captain George Cuthbert, asked General Kershaw to write General Lee. Captain Cuthbert wanted some of the men of the Second Regiment to be formed into an honor battalion because of their great fighting spirit. General Kershaw must have agreed, because he wrote General Lee a letter transmitting Captain Cuthbert's request. General Lee agreed that the performance of Kershaw's men at Fredericksburg had been unmatched. But General Lee declined to honor one battalion over another because he felt all the Confederate units were fighting with vigor and skill. Unfortunately, Captain Cuthbert, like many of the young men engaged in the war, did not live to see the bravery and courage of his, or any other, soldiers honored formally. He was killed just a few months later at Chancellorsville.

Kirkland enjoyed his short visit home. He spent time with his father, sister Caroline, several of his brothers, and, of course, his sister-in-law, Rosa. They had no way of knowing that these would be their last precious moments together. Just the same, Richard and his family cherished every minute they were together during his brief escape from the misery and death he had witnessed during the war. When Richard was not among his family, he visited his many friends and encouraged them to join the Confederate cause. Southern independence was in jeopardy, and that provided a motivating reason for them to join him.

Richard's most stirring memories of his short trip home came when he found time to court his sweetheart, Susan Evelina Kirkland, the daughter of Major Daniel Kirkland of Kershaw County. Susan and Richard were second cousins, and talked of getting married some day. It was not uncommon in 1863 for cousins to marry. Even though Susan was one of several sweethearts Richard had in Kershaw County, she was the one he spent his time with. Being with Susan helped Richard put the war out of his mind, even though it was a main topic of conversation between them.

They also talked about their future together. For the young people of the Civil War period, the future meant everything. There was so much hope for what would come -- when the war finally ended. Sadly, Richard and Susan would never see their post-war dreams come true. And when Richard stood on the porch of Major Kirkland's home telling his precious Susan good-bye, it would be the last time she would ever see him. On the top step of her father's home, Susan kissed Richard Kirkland tenderly and sent him back to the battlefield. That good-bye would last forever, but she would carry the memory of that day with her always.

Richard reluctantly left Camden, but was anxious to return to his beloved regiment. His peaceful, temporary exile from the war was interrupted outside Chancellorsville before sunrise on April 29, 1863. The soldiers were stirred by the frightening roll of the drums. The men of Kershaw moved quickly to the march, knowing battle would soon follow.

By 7:30 that morning, artillery and rifle fire nearby declared the coming attack. However, with the exception of a few skirmishes, Kershaw's Brigade did not engage the enemy that day. They remained in position at a place called Lee's Hill until midnight the next night, April 30th, when they were commanded to take up a new position near two roads called the Orange Plank Road and Turnpike. On May 1st and 2nd, the men of Kershaw's Brigade pressed the Union troops continuously, driving them from their positions.

Just before dark on the 3rd of May, they made their hardest charge near the same Hazel Run creek that had been important to them at Fredericksburg. The signal to attack was three gun shots fired rapidly and in succession. Then they charged, moving through thick brush and over fences to challenge the enemy. All the time, the enemy fired on them. Kirkland again fought the battle bravely and emerged unscathed. He and his friends fought with determination, charging with the piercing Rebel yell to push them on. The Rebel yell was now a common image of the war. It must have been a frightening sound to the Union soldiers, especially after night fell. The battle at Chancellorsville did not end at dark like most battles did. The opposing troops continued to fight into the night. The Union army was mostly in retreat, but did not leave without a fierce struggle. The Confederates pursued, determined to make their victory convincing. Men fought in hand to hand combat, unable to see who they were fighting. Sometimes Union soldiers even fought Union soldiers, and Confederates engaged Confederates. The battle continued late into the night, and Kershaw continued to maneuver his men into fighting positions until 4:00 in the morning, when they finally rested.

A severe rain storm over the next two days brought the fighting to a standstill. On the morning of May 6th, the Second Regiment found itself in the middle of a furious artillery engagement. The Second Regiment didn't try to support the fighting, but spent all their energy just shielding themselves from the barrage of shells.

The Federal soldiers fought valiantly, but the determination of the Rebel soldiers led to another great victory for General Lee's Army of Northern Virginia. General Kershaw said later that he had never been more satisfied with the conduct of his men at any time during the war than at Chancellorsville.

The defense of Virginia was successful, but costly, for General Lee. He had lost many good men. His greatest loss was General Stonewall Jackson, who was struck by one of his own men while maneuvering after dark. General Jackson held on for more than a week, but died of his wounds near the place where he had been hit. It was a great loss for the Confederacy and a great personal loss for General Lee.

Robert E. Lee was tired of fighting on his own home soil. His beloved Virginia had been ravaged by one battle after another, even though he won those battles. The victory at Chancellorsville gave Lee and the Confederate politicians great confidence, notwithstanding the tragic loss of General Jackson and many other good men. General Lee and his leaders decided it was time to take the offensive and move North to invade the Union on its own soil. Lee wanted to break down the confidence of the Union army by invading the Northern states again. He also wanted to relieve his beloved homeland of the wear and tear of war for a time, and find food for his men on the undisturbed farms of Pennsylvania.

Lee marched his troops across the Potomac River, through Maryland and into Pennsylvania. The Union army was able to keep track of the Confederate movement because the loyal citizens of Maryland and Pennsylvania would tell the Union generals when the Southern troops passed through their towns.

The Confederates were as strong as ever, and confident of victory. But they had lost many of their men in battle. To make matters worse, some of the boys from the Southern states left the army when General Lee moved into the Northern states. Those Confederate soldiers who stayed back had joined up to defend their homelands and their lives in the South. But they did not want to attack the Northern states. Other soldiers, tired and hungry, straggled behind and could not keep up with the army.

But this didn't stop General Lee. He reorganized his entire Army of Northern Virginia and marched on, in the direction of a small town in lower Pennsylvania called Gettysburg. He only intended to gather his army at Gettysburg and did not expect to do battle there.

General Kershaw marched his troops with General McLaws' Division. On July 1st, they took up a position on a road two miles from Gettysburg. The great battle had already started, almost by accident. A Union cavalry unit had ridden to Gettysburg in pursuit of the Confederate army and took up defensive positions there. When the Confederate soldiers tried to advance into the town in search of shoes and food, they met the waiting Union cavalry. What started out to be a skirmish turned into a great, bloody battle. It would be the most decisive battle of the entire war. Gettysburg would be the turning point. If the Southerners won, perhaps the war would be over. But if the Union was victorious, Lee's invasion would be turned back without achieving his goals.

On the first day of the battle, July 1, 1863, the Confederates pushed the Union troops back, out of the town and into the hills outside of Gettysburg. The Federals lost ground, but turned their retreat into an advantage by fortifying themselves on the slopes outside of the town. The battle was similar to Fredericksburg in that respect, only the Union army defended the high ground this time, and the Confederates would have to try and dislodge them.

Thousands of Confederate troops were jammed onto the roads leading to Gettysburg when the fighting starting. Longstreet's entire corps was advancing as quickly as possible to the town. Richard Kirkland and his unit were still on the march when the battle started, and would not see action at Gettysburg until the second day of the great encounter, on July 2nd.

At 4:00 that morning, Kershaw's Brigade received the order to move out. They formed quickly and energetically, finally starting their march about sunrise. They marched hard all morning in scorching heat, finally getting to the outskirts of Gettysburg about noon. They moved to a hill overlooking Gettysburg, then to the protection of a stone bridge in the afternoon.

Longstreet's Corps, which including McLaws' Division and Kershaw's Brigade, was ordered to attack the left flank of the Union army and then drive toward the middle of the Federal line. Longstreet marched his divisions in the early afternoon and was nearly in position to fight, but noticed that much of his corps was in view of the Union soldiers on the hills South of Gettysburg. To avoid being seen by the enemy, Longstreet ordered a dramatic countermarch that took the entire corps between two hills. He lost valuable time, but still established a good fighting position by mid-afternoon.

McLaws' Division encountered a murderous assault by Union troops positioned in the peach orchard and wheat field. Union General Dan Sickles had brought his men down from the hills to meet the Confederates on level ground. Just to the right of McLaws, General John Bell Hood of Texas would attack Union positions on the famous hills called Devil's Den and Little Round Top.

Kershaw's Brigade positioned itself near the peach orchard, which was occupied by the enemy. It was 4:00 in the afternoon. Kershaw's goal was to defeat the Union troops in the peach orchard and wheat field and assist in taking the Little Round Top, which would give Longstreet a chance to command the high ground on the Union left flank. Possession of Little Round Top was more important than anyone would ever know, but determined Union soldiers stood between the

Confederate troops and the Little Round Top. The Union soldiers were ordered to hold their ground at all costs.

Kershaw's troops joined thousands of other Confederate soldiers in sweeping through the peach orchard. They then faced the Union's strongest line, positioned behind a stone fence across a wheat field from the Confederate troops. Richard Kirkland and his Second Regiment, under the command of Colonel Kennedy, were ordered to engage the enemy directly in front of them, at the enemy's strongest point on its left flank.

The day was brutally hot. Even the shade of the peach orchard didn't help much. General Sickles' Union troops met Kershaw's and the other brigades in the wheat field. Kirkland charged with his comrades and pounded the Federals positioned in a strong defensive line. Fierce, bloody fighting took place in the wheat field. Soon, the Southerners overran General Sickles' men and pushed toward their goal, the hills of Little Round Top and Big Round Top, where Union troops were dug in and ready.

While Kershaw's men held the captured ground at the wheat field and the peach orchard, General Hood's men of Longstreet's Corps charged up a rocky cliff called Devil's Den. Devil's Den was an appropriate name. It was lined with boulders and was just below Little Round Top. The Confederate soldiers who eventually made it to Devil's Den pushed on to engage the Union troops on slopes of Little Round Top. But the Union lines held because of a brave, desperate defense by a handful of determined Federal soldiers. Back in the wheat field and peach orchard, Kershaw's men held their positions, despite fierce counterattacks from the Union soldiers.

Kirkland's Confederate comrades from Hood's Division eventually made it to the foot of Little Round Top, but could not advance to the top. The Union flank was protected by Colonel Joshua Lawrence Chamberlain, the same man who had fought below Marye's

Heights at Fredericksburg. Chamberlain too had helped the Union soldiers dying on the frozen hill below the stone wall at Fredericksburg. Chamberlain and young Richard Kirkland shared many personal attributes. Chamberlain ordered his men on Little Round Top to build a stone wall for protection and defense. It gave his men an advantage much like the stone wall had for the Confederates at Fredericksburg.

The Battle of Gettysburg might have been won by the Confederates if they could have taken possession of Little Round Top. At one point, only a few hundred Union soldiers held the small mountain and fought fearlessly while Confederate troops climbed the rocks or charged up the wooded slopes on other parts of the hill, nearly reaching the top.

It was a daring move by Colonel Chamberlain that held the hill for the Union. The Southerners got close to overrunning Little Round Top. Chamberlain's men were nearly out of ammunition so the colonel ordered his men to fix their bayonets. That done, Chamberlain's men charged down the hill and directly at the advancing Southerners, forcing them to retreat and many to surrender. Chamberlain's bold move saved the hill, and maybe the war, for the Union.

Back in the peach orchard, Kershaw's men held their ground. They repelled several fierce counter-strikes by the Federal forces, fighting late into the night again before they camped near the wheat field. The next day, they held their position there but were not engaged. Across the battlefield, General Lee could not break the Union lines. When Little Round Top was heavily reinforced by the Union army, the Confederates were forced to fall back from it.

On July 3rd, General Lee ordered the famous "Pickett's Charge," an all-out charge by the fresh troops of General George Pickett on the center of the Union line. It was a spirited, bloody assault by the brave men of Generals Pickett, Johnston Pettigrew and Isaac Trimble, who led three divisions into battle under the command of General Longstreet. The night before, General Lee had gone to Longstreet to ask that his most trusted commander lead the most important battle of the war. Longstreet was opposed to the attack because he did not believe it would be successful. As a faithful soldier and out of respect for General Lee, Longstreet led the all-out charge on the strong Union line at Gettysburg.

Richard Kirkland and the rest of Kershaw's Brigade held their positions near the peach orchard, but did not engage the enemy. They no doubt had mixed emotions as they watched three divisions of the Army of Northern Virginia prepare to charge the fortified Union positions. Had Kershaw's Brigade engaged that day, surely many of them would have died, like so many of their brothers who marched into a slaughter against the strong Union army. It must have been difficult for Kershaw's men and the rest of the Southern army to wait in reserve, unable to offer any assistance to their brave friends which made up "Pickett's Charge."

July 3rd was another hot day. Even the occasional rain didn't cool the heat, which was made hotter by the intensity of the battle. The opposing armies showered each other with cannon fire to try and weaken their enemies. Then, in the early afternoon, thousands of soldiers in the three Confederate divisions charged unprotected across the open fields in front of the Federal positions. Confederate soldiers fell by the hundreds, including a number of colonels and generals.

Despite the odds against them, the Confederates pushed ahead. Many never made it out of the open field, but died where they marched. Some managed to reach a stone wall where the Union had built its first line of defense. The Confederates who made it that far engaged in hand to hand combat and never moved any farther. Finally, those fortunate enough to survive the charge returned to the Southern camps in defeat.

General Lee hoped the great charge would give him a convincing victory, which would end the Battle of Gettysburg and, ultimately, the war. Instead, the attack failed. At dusk on July 3rd, the proud Confederate army was devastated and General Lee knew he had just one choice -- to fall back into Virginia.

Even though Kershaw's men did not engage the enemy on the third day, they had served with distinction at Gettysburg. They had helped carry out the spirited assault on the reinforced Union positions during the second day of the battle. They carried out every order with courage and determination. The men of Kershaw's Brigade and others fighting in the wheat field, peach orchard, and at the foot of Little Round Top had been within a few feet, and perhaps a few minutes, of turning the battle in favor of the Confederacy. But even though they got close to overrunning the Union defenses, they were unable to gain the high ground.

Until the repulse by the Union on the third day, neither side could claim victory at Gettysburg. Only after the failed Confederate charge on July 3rd were the Federals able to claim victory, forcing the Southerners to accept defeat. The Federal line had held back the charge of the Confederates. The Southern army would never again make a threat on Union soil.

Sergeant Richard Kirkland fought bravely at Gettysburg in the middle of some of the fiercest fighting of the war. More than 600 of Kershaw's men were either killed or wounded at Gettysburg. At times, Kirkland fought hand-to-hand with his brothers from the North. He impressed General Kershaw so much that Kershaw shortly promoted him to lieutenant after for his fine service at Gettysburg.

It's a miracle that Richard Kirkland was not killed or wounded at Gettysburg, where so many boys, young men and seasoned veterans fought and died. It would be the greatest battle of the war. Lee and his soldiers had hoped Gettysburg would be the last battle -- the fight that would end the war. Perhaps a Southern victory would have ended the war, but Richard Kirkland and his friends had no time to think about that. They were forced to resume the march South. They would never know how close they were to winning the war -- how close they were to never fighting again. Only a few feet of ground at the top of Little Round Top, earth and dirt that was within the grasp of Kirkland's peers, cost the Confederates a chance to end the war. Richard Kirkland was perhaps a few feet away from surviving the war. A Confederate victory at Gettysburg might have spared him the danger of fighting in other battles. But fate was not on the side of the Southern army, or Richard Kirkland, and at Gettysburg, he used up the last of his good luck.

Just like at Fredericksburg, Richard Kirkland and Colonel Joshua Chamberlain of the Union army fought almost face-to-face. They were both compassionate, courageous soldiers, so much alike, although they would never meet. Kirkland forged his name into history at Fredericksburg. Chamberlain would become famous for his daring acts at Gettysburg, being awarded the Congressional Medal of Honor for his brave defense of Little Round Top. He would later become the governor of Maine, and a well-known scholar. Richard Kirkland's lasting contribution on the hill at Marye's Heights would have to stand alone. That would be his one act of fame.

Like Daniel of old in the lion's den,
He walked through the murderous air
With never a breath of the leaden storm
To touch or to tear his gray-clad form.
For the hand of God was there.

Miraculously, Richard Kirkland survived Gettysburg without a scratch, even though it was the bloodiest battle ever fought on American soil. The failure at Gettysburg hurt the morale of the Confederate troops, for many had thought and hoped Gettysburg would be the last battle. It would only become the midway, and the turning, point of the long and brutal War Between the States. For the exhausted and battered troops of General Kershaw's Brigade, there was no time to rest and allow their wounds to heal. Immediately following the third day of the battle, the Confederate soldiers began a disheartening retreat back into Virginia. Then, just days after the battle, Kershaw's Brigade was ordered to help defend the Confederacy's western front, which had been broken at Vicksburg, Mississippi. Help was needed in Tennessee and Georgia. So the entire corps of General Longstreet, which included Kershaw's Brigade, was sent South.

The tired, but determined gray-clad soldiers boarded trains in Virginia and traveled through North Carolina and South Carolina. All along the way, Kirkland and all the Confederate soldiers were cheered as heroes. During their scheduled stops along the way, the citizens took the Southern troops into their homes and served up large, tasty meals. The fattest turkey or chicken was killed, cooked, and served to these heroes of the Confederacy. The fatigue of travel was softened by the joyous reception given the war-battered soldiers. They were back in their homeland, at least for a few days, and it was a tiring, but entertaining trip. Unfortunately, these would be Richard Kirkland's last joyful moments. His last good experience was being promoted to lieutenant by General Kershaw.

Kershaw and his men, which included Lieutenant Richard Kirkland, arrived in Georgia in mid-September to assist the Southern army already engaged with Union troops near Chattanooga, Tennessee. Union soldiers were in nearby Chattanooga and trying to move east. Just a few miles from Chattanooga, in Northern Georgia, they positioned their army. Near a sluggish creek the Cherokee Indians called Chickamauga, the River of Death, the Union army waited for the Confederate soldiers to attack.

During the fierce, bloody two-day battle, the small stream would live up to its name, for blood on both sides would be freely spilled into the River of Death. Before the two great armies waged battle here, Chickamauga was just like most areas that would become Civil War battlefields -- a quiet, hilly and peaceful farm region. The grass was bright green and the forests thickly wooded. It was a peaceful region, much like the plush farmland that surrounded Gettysburg.

Fighting began on September 19th, but Kershaw's men did not arrive in time to participate in the battle on the first day. They had actually arrived in Georgia at midnight on September 18th and paraded toward the battlefield the next day. They marched across the

Chickamauga at a place called Alexander's Bridge and made camp again at about 1:00 on the morning of September 20th.

When the sun came up on September 20th, Kershaw's Brigade was ordered to stand ready for combat. By 11:00 that morning, Kershaw's men had positioned themselves in the rear of General John Hood's division. Hood's men charged through a forest and, when they emerged from the woods, became involved in a fierce struggle that drove many of the Confederates' first line back into Kershaw's advancing line. The Confederates pushed back. The battle would go back and forth like that all day. At one moment, it would appear that the Union had gained the upper hand, and would drive the Southern armies from the battlefield. But then the Confederates would regroup and charge again with their loud, hearty cheer and would drive the Union soldiers into a temporary retreat.

McLaws' Division, which included Kershaw's Brigade and Richard Kirkland's Second Regiment, were thrust into the center of the Union line near a place called Snodgrass Hill. Kirkland fought fearlessly and, with his comrades, made a strong charge on the Union lines at Snodgrass Hill in the early afternoon. They made a murderous assault, shouting and fighting as they overran the Union position. The air was filled with smoke from cannon and rifle fire. The smoke was so thick that at times the soldiers couldn't see the enemy in front of them, a hundred feet away. There didn't seem to be enough air to breath, with all the smoke, and thousands of men on the field, standing face to face in a fight to the death. This time, the Union troops could not hold, and Kirkland and his comrades captured Union artillery and even the Union headquarters at a home called the Widow Glenn's House. But then the Union soldiers were reinforced, and Kershaw would be forced to pull his men back. It was like many battles. It was hard at times to tell who was winning. And an army only declared itself the winner when the enemy gave up the ground it was holding and retreated to safer ground. That would finally happen on this day, but not until the battle waged back and forth, and many good men and boys had fallen on the grassy hills in North Georgia.

At one point, Kershaw and his units fell back a few hundred yards, and the Union soldiers thought the brigade was retreating. The Union army continued to attack, but the Confederates held their new position and waited for reinforcements. Kirkland and the Second Regiment were given the responsibility of holding the Union army off until help arrived. General Kershaw called this one of the most gallant struggles by his men that he had ever seen. He was determined to hold the enemy until support came. But the Union soldiers advanced. By cool, deliberate and accurate fire, the men of Kershaw halted the advance and when their reinforcements arrived, Kershaw's Brigade made a last furious charge at Snodgrass Hill. With hearty cheers, the South Carolina Second and Third Regiments engaged the enemy with great enthusiasm.

The Second Regiment made one of the fastest and most successful dashes, pushing up the hill and onto the crest, the objective which the Southern generals wanted their armies to reach. Even when the Union soldiers tried to push the Confederates back, the Second Regiment fought vigorously to hold the ground they had worked so hard to gain. The Union army did make small advances. But most of their movement was in the direction of Chattanooga.

It was toward the end of this day that Richard Kirkland met the awful fate that came to many of the brave young men who served. During one of the last charges, Kirkland and his friends broke through a Union line and met solid reinforcements. The Second South Carolina was forced into a temporary retreat when they could not hold the ground where the Union reinforcements stood. Still, Kershaw's men maintained the overall advantage. And they would soon press the advantage. But for a few minutes, they were forced back to a safer fighting position.

Kirkland and two of his comrades, Ario Niles and James Arrants, were in the front of the Confederate line when they found themselves exposed on a grassy knoll. Arrants and Niles quickly turned back to seek safer ground, but Kirkland insisted on facing the enemy and firing at the advancing Union troops to cover his friends while they took cover. Niles and Arrants begged Kirkland not to stand against the charging enemy troops. But Richard Kirkland's courage and complete unselfishness guided his actions, and he stood against the surge of the enemy and defended the troops in his unit. While engaging the charging Union soldiers, Kirkland was shot in the chest and fell mortally wounded.

Niles and Arrants tried to carry him from the field, but Kirkland knew they would be putting themselves in danger by staying behind with him.

"No, I am done for," Richard Kirkland told his friends. Blood poured from his mouth and the nasty wound in his chest. "You can do me no good. Save yourselves. Tell Pa I died right. I died at my post."

Those were the last words of Richard Rowland Kirkland, *The Angel of Marye's Heights*. He was barely twenty years old.

In a cruel twist of fate, only a few minutes later, the Confederates reformed their line and returned to the offensive. The Southern army fought fiercely until sundown and recaptured the lost ground. Kirkland's Second Regiment fought on without him, finally driving the Union army from the field and back to Chattanooga. The Second Regiment was the last of Kershaw's regiments to retire from the fight.

Richard Kirkland's body was then removed from the battlefield. He was one of many casualties at Chickamauga. Half of Kershaw's

Brigade were either killed or wounded there, and many more South Carolina boys died on the battlefield. Hundreds of young soldiers were buried in shallow graves on the battlefield. Richard Kirkland's body was sent back to his family in Kershaw County, where it was buried in a secluded spot on the family's White Oak plantation. His grave was marked with a simple wounded stake carved with the initials, *R.R.K.*

Lieutenant Richard Kirkland forged his way into history with one singular act of compassion and courage. His extraordinary deed at Marye's Heights during the Battle of Fredericksburg was preserved by a handful of officers and soldiers who recognized this event as a mirror of the kind of soldier he was, and the kind of life he lived.

The Southern army fought on, as it did each time it lost one of its heroes. It's only a coincidence that after Richard Kirkland was gone, the South never enjoyed the sweet success of victory on the battlefield. Richard Kirkland had been a part of nearly every great triumph by his army. If he had walked away from the battlefield at Chickamauga, he would have never tasted victory again. But he might have survived, returned to his family, and received the reward, richly deserved, of his labors and sacrifice. He would have heard his friends and family call him a hero.

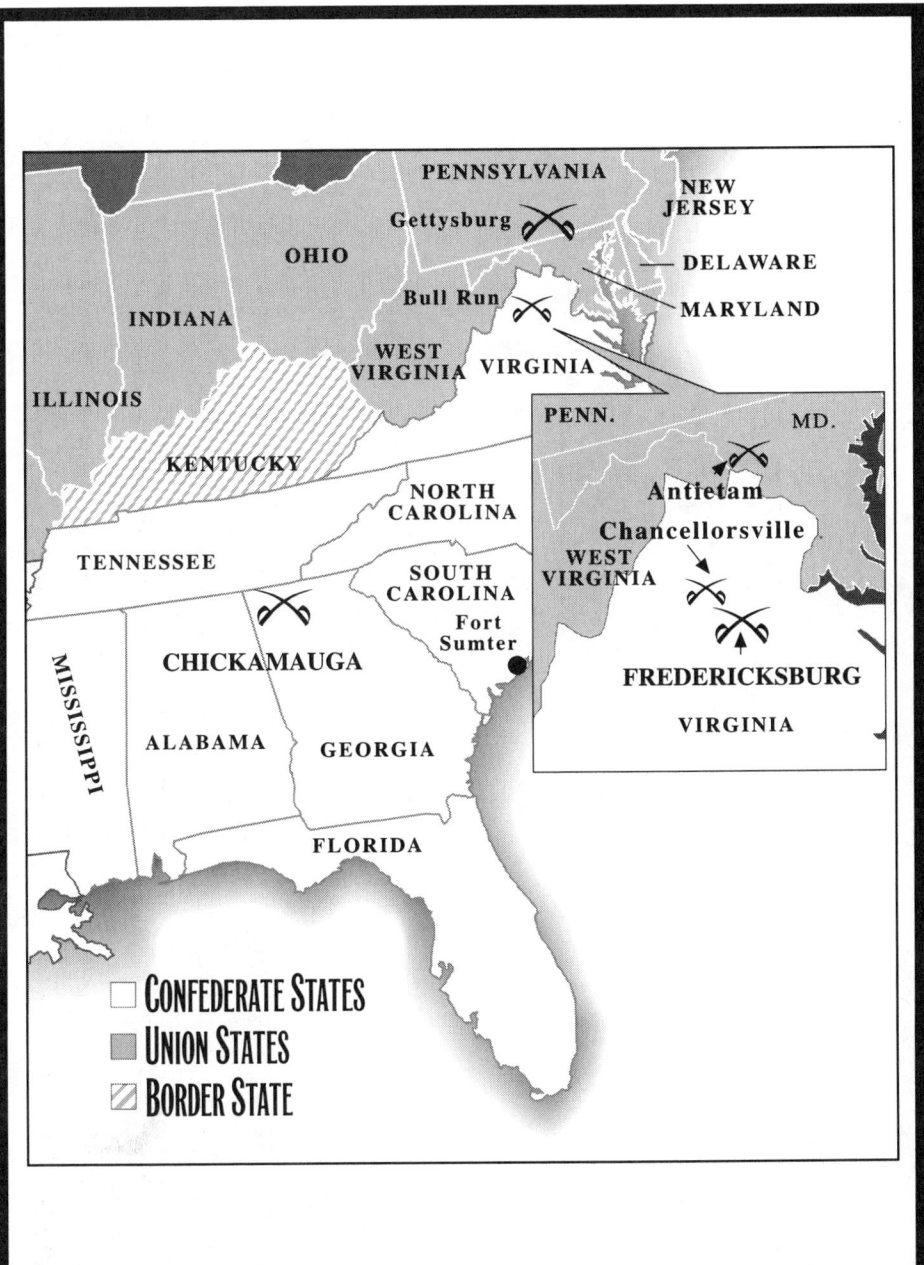

Map of the Battlefields.

The Richard Kirkland tomb in Camden, South Carolina.

" And I am sure in the Book of Gold,
Where the blessed angel writes
The names that are blessed of God and men
He wrote that day with his shining pen,
Then smiled and lovingly wrote again:
'The Angel of Marye's Heights.'"

Epilogue

Richard Kirkland never led an army into battle. He never engineered a great victory on the battlefield. But he was a Civil War hero just the same. He joined the Confederate army because he felt it was his duty to protect the freedoms his ancestors had fought so long to gain. Until his death at Chickamauga, he fought bravely, always carried out every order, always performed his duty with loyalty and courage. His last act at Chickamauga was brave and unselfish. He put his life in danger to protect his friends while they retreated from the enemy. He ultimately gave his life to defend the men fighting with him.

Richard Kirkland was like thousands of other young men who fought on both sides, the Union and the Confederacy. More than death, they feared losing what they had. In many ways, Richard Kirkland was no different than the rest of those who fought with him, and who fought against him. But he was just a little different. He loved his homeland, but he had compassion for those who fought against him. And one singular, noble act of bravery and compassion separated him from all the others. His one unrehearsed act of mercy has caused the name of Richard Kirkland to be preserved. It transformed him from an ordinary soldier to an extraordinary soldier.

But Kirkland's mission of mercy at Fredericksburg was not well known. Certainly, it did not go unnoticed by those who witnessed it. The Union soldiers who watched the Confederate sergeant comfort their fallen comrades cheered him. They called him the Angel of Marye's Heights.

But Richard Kirkland's name is just briefly mentioned in the history books, in other biographies, and rarely in the official reports of the war. Those volumes list the people who were responsible for winning and losing battles. Richard Kirkland's name rarely appears there. Thankfully, though, people told Richard Kirkland's story, even though no one wrote it down for many years. Gradually, the story was nearly forgotten.

General Kershaw led his brigade into other battles after Kirkland's death at Chickamauga. He continued to polish his reputation as a noble leader. General Lee said that Kershaw kept his poise during times of strife. Kershaw was said to pass through hazards unvexed. And even when his troops were surrounded and the war lost, he maintained his dignity. Kershaw was captured in the closing days of the war, and was not with Lee during the Confederate surrender at Appomattox Courthouse on April 9, 1865. Even after the surrender, Kershaw spent several months in prison.

General Kershaw, who eventually became a major general and division commander, returned to Kershaw County after the war. He resumed his law career and was eventually elected to the state circuit court. He retired in 1883 and died the next year.

But Kershaw never forgot the memorable days at Fredericksburg and the young man who helped make that battle unforgettable for everyone in sight of Kirkland -- Union soldiers still fighting from Fredericksburg, Confederates crowded on the muddy Sunken Road, and above it at Marye's Heights. Perhaps Kirkland's story would have remained just a legend, only passed down word-of-mouth by the men who witnessed young Richard's compassionate act. But General Joseph B. Kershaw kept the legend alive. In 1880, Kershaw put the tale into history when he wrote an account of Fredericksburg for the *News and Courier* in Charleston, South Carolina. Kershaw not only told the story, but described the kind of person capable of performing such an act.

General Kershaw emphasized one very important fact -- that it was not only extraordinary what Richard Kirkland did at Fredericksburg, but that the young sergeant performed his great act of mercy almost certain he would be killed while going to the aid of the fallen Union soldiers. But that didn't matter to him. He was willing to make the sacrifice.

Kirkland's story was read by some, and occasionally reprinted. But it took another two or three decades before Kirkland's name began to appear in the history books used in schools.

Colonel W. D. Trantham paid further tribute to Kirkland in a Memorial Day speech in 1899. During his address, Trantham, who was with Kirkland at Chickamauga, told how Richard Kirkland fought bravely, and died with honor. Trantham spoke proudly of Kirkland:

The circumstances of his death were most heroic.
He fought literally until the last gasp, and in the very
presence and moment of death showed that the sublime

self-sacrifice and regard for others which he exhibited at Fredericksburg, was a settled principle of his nature."

Kirkland was loved and honored by his young contemporaries as well, including his pal T. M. Rembert of Company E, Second Regiment. Rembert and Kirkland were together in many battles. Years after the war, from his home in Ridgeway, South Carolina, Rembert penned a brief tribute to his dear friend. The short narrative was published in the *Confederate Veteran* in 1903.

"Richard Kirkland belonged to Company E, Second Regiment, South Carolina Volunteers. He was at the siege of Fort Sumter, and went from there to Virginia, and was in the battles of Manassas. The incident referred to occurred at Fredericksburg, and shows how he was actuated by feelings of pure humanity.

"(The Union) dead and dying for hundreds of yards in our front were literally piled on each other, and the cries of the wounded for water were distressing. The heart of the noble and brave Richard Kirkland, a mere boy, could stand it no longer. He left our lines and went to the brave and peerless Kershaw...Kershaw refused, and told him he would surely be killed; but the noble boy insisted, and Kershaw at last consented.

"The enemy saw him, and supposing his purpose was to rob the dead and wounded, rained shot and shell upon the brave Samaritan. God took care of him. Soon he lifted the head of one of the wounded enemy, placed the canteen to his lips, and cooled his burning thirst. His motivation was then seen and the fire silenced. Shout

> *after shout went up from friend and foe alike in honor of this brave deed.*
>
> *"I knew this brave boy; he was my friend and chum; we shared each other's blankets. He was a noble boy...He fought through all the Virginia battles in Longstreet's Corps, and was killed on the bloody field of Chickamauga...He did his duty and always answered the roll call. No nobler soul ever winged its flight from the field of battle than that of Richard Kirkland...Sleep on, dear friend. Your old comrades will soon join you in your home of rest."*

Another colleague, William H. Whitmire, added this brief reference in his recollections of the war, titled *Reminiscence*. Of Kirkland, he wrote:

> *"We were on the Heights of Marye at the foot of which was the `Sunken Road,' separating us from the enemy. Here they (Union soldiers) were caught, and as they lay dying, young Richard Kirkland, a brave South Carolina lad, risking his life, carried water to their parching lips."*

In 1909, a request was made to move the remains of Richard Kirkland from his family's small cemetery on White Oak Creek to the Quaker Cemetery in Camden. He had rested in peace for nearly a half century in the secluded spot near his birthplace. But his obscure grave marker was nearly hidden and lost, and many thought his remains should be moved to a public place, where people could come and honor Kirkland and his courageous life. His brother Dan, also a veteran of the Civil War, acted for the family in granting permission for Richard's body to be moved. In a solemn ceremony, the place of his final resting place was rededicated.

Today, his tombstone can be viewed by visitors, along with the grave markers of General Kershaw, John D. Kennedy, and other heroes from the area. The inscription on the tombstone reads:

> Richard Kirkland, CSA, who at the Battle of
> Fredericksburg, Risked his life to carry water
> to wounded and dying enemies, and at the Battle
> of Chickamauga, laid down his life for his
> Country.
>
> 1843-1863
>
> *'If thine enemy thirst, give him drink.'*

For the next year, the school children of Camden collected their pennies. In 1910, a fountain was erected in Camden to honor Kirkland. The memorial tablet reads:

> To
> Richard Kirkland
> C.S.A.
> IN COMMEMORATION OF HIS HEROISM
> AT FREDERICKSBURG, DEC. 13, 1862.
> CHRISTLIKE COMPASSION MOVED HIM
> TO LEAP OVER THE STONE WALL, A
> MARK FOR HOSTILE GUNS, AND CARRY
> WATER AGAIN AND AGAIN, TO THE

SUFFERING FOE FALLEN THICK IN
FRONT.
"Greater love hath no man than this."
HE FELL AT CHICKAMAUGA, AGED 20.
A Tribute from the school children
of Camden
A.D. 1910

In 1965, Richard Kirkland was further honored when a large, bronze sculpture was dedicated in his honor, and erected on the Fredericksburg battlefield near the Sunken Road. In 1991, the Sergeant Kirkland's Museum and Historical Society was founded. Its purpose is "to preserve by education the statements, images, and values of those early members of our society that displayed both conviction and compassion in times of great peril during this country's development." The statue presents a sensitive depiction of Kirkland giving water to the wounded Union soldiers at Fredericksburg. Thousands visit the National Park, the museum and the battlefield each year, and the name Richard Kirkland, and the deed he performed, has become better known in recent years. There is also a street in Fredericksburg named after Kirkland.

During the closing days of the war in 1865, the Confederate government was preparing a Confederate Medal of Honor for the Southern heroes of the war. The Confederate Congress, with approval of President Jefferson Davis, had passed a joint resolution establishing a Medal of Honor for the brave men of the South. However, the effort fell short when the government abandoned Richmond after the war. More than 110 years later, the effort was revitalized, and, in the mid-1970s, Richard Kirkland was nominated for the highest honor available to Confederate soldiers. His nomination was enthusiastically approved, and more than a century after his gallant act at

Fredericksburg, the Confederate Medal of Honor was awarded posthumously to Lieutenant Richard Rowland Kirkland by the Sons of Confederate Veterans. The award was dated August 17, 1977, and presented a month later to the governor of South Carolina, James B. Edwards.

Artist Robert Wilson painted a moving portrait of Richard Kirkland's compassion, also titled *The Angel of Marye's Heights*. The portrait brings to life the tenderness of Kirkland displayed so unselfishly below the Sunken Road. The painting was unveiled in 1984 and hangs in the state capitol building in Columbia, South Carolina. Immediately under the painting, encased in glass, is Richard Kirkland's Confederate Medal of Honor. Wilson's portrait was reproduced for the cover of this book.

THE ANGEL OF MARYE'S HEIGHTS

A sunken road and a wall of stone
And Cobb's grim line of gray
Lay still at the base of Marye's hill
On the morn of a winter's day.

And crowning the frowning crest above
Sleep Alexander's guns,
While gleaming fair in the sunlit air
The Rappahannock runs.

On the plains below the blue lines glow
And the bugle rings out clear,
As with bated breath they march to death
And a soldier's honored bier.

For the slumbering guns awake to life
And the screaming shell and ball
From the front and flanks crash through the ranks
And leave them where they fall.

And the gray stone wall is ringed with fire
And the pitiless leaden hail
Drives back the foe to the plain below,
Shattered and crippled and frail.

Again and again a new line forms
And the gallant charge is made,
And again and again they fall like grain
In the sweep of a reaper's blade.

And then from out of the battle smoke
There falls on the lead-swept air
From the whitening lips that are ready to die
The piteous moan and the plaintive cry
For "water" everywhere.

And into the presence of Kershaw brave
There comes a fair-faced lad
With quivering lips as his cap he tips,
"I can't stand this," he said.

Stand what? the general sternly said
As he looked on the field of slaughter,
"To see those poor boys dying out there
With no one to help them, no one to care,
And crying for water! water!'

If you'll let me go, I'll give them some.
Why, boy, you're simply mad;
They'll kill you as soon as you scale the wall
In this terrible storm of shell and ball,
The general kindly said.

Please let me go, the lad replied.
May the Lord protect you, then!
And over the wall in the hissing air
He carried comfort to grim despair
And balm to the stricken men.

And, as he straightened their mangled limbs
On their earthen bed of pain,
The whitening lips all eagerly quaffed
From the canteen's mouth the cooling draught
And blessed him again and again.

Like Daniel of old in the lion's den,
He walked through the murderous air
With never a breath of the leaden air
To touch or to tear his gray-clad form,
For the hand of God was there.

And I am sure in the Book of Gold,
Where the blessed angel writes
The names that are blessed of God and men
He wrote that day with his shining pen
Then smiled and lovingly wrote again,
The Angel of Marye's Heights.

-- Walter A. Clark, 1908

The Richard Rowland Kirkland Memorial at Fredericksburg, Virginia.

Index

22nd South Carolina Militia. 4
2nd Palmetto Regiment . . 10
Alexander's Bridge 66
Anderson, Robert 11
Antietam Campaign . . 27, 29
Appomattox Courthouse . 74
Army of Northern
   Virginia . . . 31, 56, 58, 62
Army of the Potomac . . . 32
Arrants, James. 69
Barksdale 28
Battle of Fredericksburg. . 35
Beauregard, Pierre G. T. . 11
Bee, Barnard E. 18
Bull Run. . . . . . . ii, 17, 18
Burnside, Ambrose . . 32-34,
   . . . . 38, 40, 51
Camden . 3, 5, 7, 9, 55, 77-79
Camden Volunteers . . . 9, 10
Camp McLaws 24
Chain Carriers. 5
Chamberlain, Joshua
   Lawrence . v, 39, 60, 61, 64
Chancellorsville 54-57
Charleston 13, 16
Chattanooga 66, 68, 69
Chickahominy River . . . 25
Chickamauga . . . 26, 66, 69,
   . . . . . . 70, 73-75, 77-79
Citadel. 13
Cobb, Thomas R. R.. . . .34-37
Columbia 7
Company E, Second
   Regiment, South Carolina
   Volunteers, Infantry . . . 9,
   . . . . 27, 76
Company G, Second
   Regiment, South Carolina
   Volunteers, Infantry . . . 27
Confederate Medal
   of Honor 79, 80
Confederate States
   of America 2, 17, 18
Confederate Veteran 76
Congressional Medal
   of Honor 64
Cuthbert, George 54
Davis, Jefferson. 79
Devil's Den 59, 60
Doby 38
Elk Ridge 28
Flat Rock 5, 24, 25
Flat Rock Guards 9, 27
Flat Rock Township . . . 2, 5
Fort Sumter . . ii, 4, 10-13, 76
Fredericksburg . . . ii, vi, 26,
   . . . . . 30-32, 34, 40, 49,
   . . . . . 51, 53, 54, 56, 58,
   . . . . 60, 61, 64, 70,
   . . . . 74-76, 78, 79
Gettysburg ii, 39, 58, 59, 61-66
Grant, Ulysses S. v
Gum Swamp 5, 7
Harper's Ferry 27
Hazel Run. 33, 36, 56
Henry House Hill 18
Hood, John Bell . . 59, 60, 67
Jackson, Thomas
   "Stonewall" . . v, 18, 33, 57

Index

James River 23
Kennedy, John Doby . . 9, 10,
. . . . 27, 29, 37, 44, 60, 77
Kershaw, Joseph B. . . 9, 12, 13,
. . . . 17, 18, 29, 35, 37, 38,
. . . . . 40, 44-48, 51, 54-56,
. . . . . 58-63, 66-69, 74-77
Kershaw County. . . i-3, 5, 6,
. . . . 9-11, 14, 37, 53,
. . . . 55, 70, 74
Kershaw's Brigade . . 27, 30,
. . . . 31, 33, 35, 51, 54-56,
. . . . . 59, 62, 63, 65, 67-69
Kirkland
  Billy 4, 22, 24
  Caroline 3, 54
  Dan . . . 3, 4, 22, 24, 25, 77
  Daniel 55
  James 4, 6, 7
  Jesse 4, 14, 21
  John A. 3, 6, 7
  Mary Vaughn 3
  Rosa 21, 22, 24, 54
  Sam 4, 7, 24, 25
  Susan Evelina 55
Kirkwood Rangers . 4, 9, 22,
. . . . 24, 25
Lee, Robert E. . . . . . v, 29, 30,
. . . . 32-34, 45, 51, 54,
. . . . 56-58, 61-63, 74
Lee's Hill 35, 55
Lincoln, Abraham . . . 18, 32,
. . . . 40, 51
Little Round Top 59-61, 63, 64
Longstreet, James . . . . v, 36,
. . . . 58-62, 65, 77
Lynches River 6
Manassas Junction . 17, 18, 76
Marye's Heights . . 34-39, 51,
. . 53, 60, 64, 70, 74, 75, 77
Maryland Heights 28
McClellan. 32
McLaws. 29
Lafayette 36, 58, 59, 67
Mitchell's Ford 17
Morris Island 10, 12, 14
News and Courier 75
Niles, Ario 69
Orange Plank Road and
  Turnpike 56
Petersburg 13
Pettigrew, Johnston 61
Pickens, Governor
  Francis W. 2
Pickett, George 61
Pickett's Charge 61, 62
Point Lookout 4
Potomac River 57
Quaker Cemetery 77
Rappahannock River . . 32, 33
Rebel yell 18, 56
Rembert, T. M. . 26, 40, 51, 76
Reminiscence 77
Richmond . . . 13, 14, 17, 21,
. . . . 32, 79
Second South Carolina
  Regiment . . . 17, 27-29, 33,
  . . . . 36, 54, 56, 60, 67-69
Sergeant Kirkland's Museum
  and Historical Society . . 79

Seven Days' Battles . . 21, 27
Seventh South Carolina
   Cavalry 4
Sharpsburg 27-29
Sherman, William T. . . . 6, 7
Sibley 26
Sickles, Dan 59, 60
Sill, John. 5
Snodgrass Hill. 67, 68
Sons of Confederate
   Veterans 79
South Carolina General
   Assembly 1
South Carolina Military
   Academy. 2
Spotsylvania Court House. 34
Stevens House. . . 36, 38, 44

Stover, David 22
Sunken Road 34-38, 75,
   . . . . 77, 79, 80
Telegraph Road. 34-36
Third South Carolina
   Regiment 35, 36, 68
Trantham, W. D. 51, 75
Trimble, Isaac 61
Truesdel, Billy . 21, 22, 24, 25
Vicksburg. 65
Washington 16, 17, 32
West Point 2
White Oak 70, 77
Whitmire, William H. . . . 77
Widow Glenn's House . . . 67
Wilmington 13

Les Carroll received a Journalism degree from Brigham Young University and worked briefly as a newspaper reporter before joining the United States Air Force. He served four and a half years and then transferred to the South Carolina National Guard, where he works as public affairs director. He lives in Columbia, South Carolina with his wife, Suzanne, and their five children. ***The Angel of Marye's Heights*** is his first book.

RICHLAND COUNTY PUBLIC LIBRARY

3 0080 01468 9430

```
    973.73 Car

Carroll, Les.
The angel of Marye's
Heights : Sergeant Richard
30080014689430    1500    M
```

31

RICHLAND COUNTY PUBLIC LIBRARY
COLUMBIA, SOUTH CAROLINA 29201

OCT 2 6 1994